THE HERITAGE OF

CLONMACNOISE

Environmental Sciences Unit, Trinity College
in association with
County Offaly Vocational Educational Committee

First published in 1987 by the Environmental
Sciences Unit, Trinity College in association
with County Offaly Vocational Educational
Committee, O'Connor Square, Tullamore,
Co. Offaly.

Managing Editor: Mary Tubridy
Text Editor: Mary Tubridy
Drawings (with the exception of Ch.7):
Harry McConville
Drawings (Ch.7): Eamonn Sinnott
Maps and Cartography: Tom McConville

ISBN 0-9512627-0-X Hardback
ISBN 0-9512627-1-8 Softback

Cataloguing and Publication Data
Tubridy, M. and Jeffrey, D. W.
The Heritage of Clonmacnoise
1. Natural History — Ireland
2. Historical Geography — Ireland

Designed by Raymond Kyne Design Associates
Typeset by Computer Graphics Ltd.
Printed by Criterion Press Ltd.
Colour Separations by Colour Repro Ltd.

Distributed by Co. Offaly Vocational
Educational Committee, O'Connor Squ
Tullamore, Co. Offaly.

Contents

Introduction

Our generation has inherited a remarkable living landscape at Clonmacnoise which is rich in cultural significance, beauty and interest. This book is a guide to all its elements including the geological past and a series of almost primeval habitats which interact with the history of man and Christianity in Europe. While the contributors are all specialists the book is written for the people of the Midlands and their visitors.

The future of this heritage lies in the careful blending of protective care and wise use that we term "conservation". We suggest the concept of coordinating the conservation of different heritage items, and doing so in a way that promotes rather than restricts economic activity and rural development. This is a new direction for conservation.

Production of the book brought together many people and ideas. The first discussion about "Heritage Zones" occurred when An Taisce was negotiating with Bord na Mona about Mongan Bog. At that time Bord Fáilte in conjunction with the Office of Public Works and Offaly County Council commissioned a planning survey of the area associated with the national monument. This survey coincided with the first EEC funded study of the Heritage Zone by the Trinity College team. When the initial findings of this study were published, Offaly County Council and Offaly Vocational Education Committee became interested in the publication of a book on the Zone which could be used by students and tourists. Publication was only possible with the encouragement and sponsorship of these two bodies together with financial support from the Electricity Supply Board, Bord na Móna and the Office of Public Works: whose help we gratefully acknowledge.

Dr. D.W. Jeffrey
Director, Clonmacnoise Heritage Zone Project

CHAPTER ONE

The Landscape of Clonmacnoise

Peter Coxon

INTRODUCTION

According to local folklore, the Clonfinlough Stone, a large carved rock lying in a field 3 km east of Clonmacnoise is the oldest stone in Ireland. This stone is also a national monument as it is thought to have received its carvings during the Bronze Age 4,500 years ago. Unfortunately, geologists have not confirmed the legend but there are numerous features in Clonmacnoise which will interest the student of rocks and landscapes. The Heritage Zone (fig. 1.1) is one of the few places east of the Shannon where one can see a large expanse of limestone, the rock which underlies the Central Plain; in places worn and pitted in patterns associated with the Burren. The prominent hills are all eskers formed in rivers which flowed under the melting ice cap which covered Clonmacnoise 20,000 years ago. Along the margin of the zone meanders the Shannon, the last large undrained river in Europe and the longest river in Britain and Ireland.

TROPICAL CLONMACNOISE

The story of the landscape starts with the formation of the rock which underlies Clonmacnoise. Clonmacnoise is located in the Central Lowlands of Ireland which covers one third of the island's surface and is underlain predominantly by limestone. This rock was formed 350 million years ago when Ireland lay close to the Equator

Fig. 1.1
Clonmacnoise Heritage
Zone showing the features
of the landscape and areas
of natural history interest.

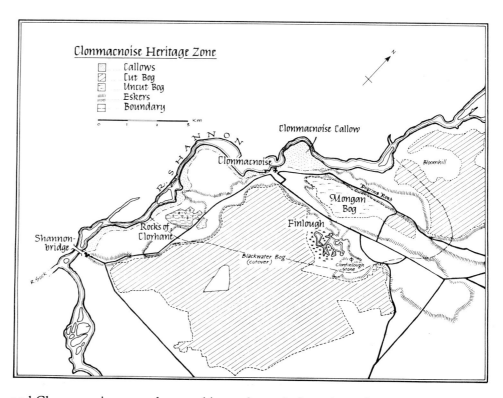

and Clonmacnoise was submerged in a sub-tropical coral sea about 100 metres deep. In this water lived sea creatures including nautiloids and trilobites, now long extinct. Many had shells similar to cockles and consisting of calcium carbonate or calcite. As they died their shells accumulated at the bottom of the sea in a soft ooze of precipitated calcite and other sedimented materials, eventually building up to a thickness of several hundred metres. Over millions of years this was consolidated by pressure to form limestone. In the limestone visible in Clonmacnoise at "The Rocks of Clorhane" (fig. 1.1), many of these fossil animals can be seen; the commonest types are "sea lily" stems ; the discs which make up the stem are the parts most commonly found as fossils (fig. 1.2).

Fig. 1.2
Sea-lilies found in Tropical
Seas resemble fossil types.
The only parts seen as
fossils in Egan's quarry near
the "Rocks of Clorhane"
are the stems.

The character of the limestone changed depending on various factors such as the depth of the sea and the distance to dry land. (The only dry land was probably found in a small part of Northern Ireland.) Much later, the layers of limestone were lifted and tilted by movements of the earth so that now, instead of having the youngest rocks on top, rocks of different ages can be seen at or near the surface in the Heritage Zone. Rocks at Bloomhill, 7 km NE of the Monument are tens of millions of years older than those found at "The Rocks of Clorhane" As the limestone at "The Rocks" was formed towards the end of the time for which the Tropical Sea covered this area it is very pure limestone and was quarried extensively in the last century. At Egan's Quarry, there are still massive blocks of limestone and half carved headstones and one can also see that the beds, originally horizontal, are tilted at an angle of 30 degrees (fig. 1.3).

Fig. 1.3
Quarrying for stone at Egan's Quarry has shown that the beds of limestone are tilted at an angle.

CLONMACNOISE DISSOLVING AWAY

If one examines the limestone at "The Rocks" or comes across it elsewhere in Ireland, (e.g. the Burren, Co. Clare) it seems to be an extremely hard rock, which one might expect to be very resistant to wear. However, the calcite of which the limestone is composed gives it a unique property: it can be dissolved. It is only slightly soluble in rainwater, but as rainwater passes through the soil, it turns into a weak acid — which dissolves the limestone more effectively. The results can be seen at "The Rocks of Clorhane" and on the patches of bare rock scattered throughout the area.

Where water has passed along the joints and the bedding planes (the divisions between the beds or layers), a pattern of fissures (called grykes) and flat areas or pavement (clints) has formed. As the limestone at "The Rocks" has been steeply tilted, the pavement forms wide openings leading down from the surface (See fig. 1.4).

The blocks of limestone between the joints and bedding planes also show signs of solution in the form of hollows and channels, called *Karren*. Their shape suggests that they formed under a cover of soil and vegetation which has since been removed.

Fig. 1.4
Limestone rock develops unusual patterns as it is dissolved away by rainwater; flat areas called clints separated by deep fissures as shown here, called grykes.

Geologically speaking, limestone solution is a rapid process and it has been calculated that (at present day rates of solution) a half metre of limestone has been removed in the past 10,000 years. Due to this prolonged solution, the limestone areas in Ireland like the Central Plain are no longer uplands except where the limestone has been overlain by a protective cap of more resistant rock.

We can imagine that Clonmacnoise had a landscape of hills and valleys made of limestone after it emerged from the sea during the Tertiary Period 65 — 2 million years ago. Dense forests covered the hillsides consisting of exotic conifers, giant redwoods, and monkey-puzzle trees. In the valleys and lowlands there were impenetrable swamps, like those in Florida today, vegetated with swamp cypress.

During the Tertiary Period, about 25 million years ago, the Earth's climate began to cool. This cooling led to the Ice Age and altered the landscape everywhere in Ireland but particularly in the Midlands. The landscape we see in Clonmacnoise is largely the result of the movement of a great ice cap which covered the area 20,000 years ago.

THE ICE AGE

Two million years ago the earth's climate (under the influence of the planet's position relative to the sun) became unstable and began to "see-saw" from cool to warm. This period is known as the Quaternary — when the climate changed from cold to warm in several cycles, leaving evidence in Northern Europe and Ireland of cold, glacial periods and intervening warmer, interglacial ones. It is thought we are still in the Quaternary Period with the prospect of another Ice Age in the future.

Fig. 1.5
The woolly mammoth was probably extinct before man arrived in Ireland but remained much longer in Siberia where carcasses have been found complete with skin and flesh buried in thick ice.

Ireland has, therefore, been affected by many ice ages but it is the legacy of the Last Glaciation — known as the Midlandian Glaciation (100,000 to 10,000 years ago) that most strongly affected the landscape. This cold period was itself a complex event with only relatively short periods of actual glacial ice cover. The maximum cover by ice occurred at about 20 - 18,000 years ago and the ice had retreated by 16,000 years ago.

Bones of mammals found in caves give a glimpse of the animal life that roamed the frozen landscape during the Last Glaciation. Wolf, stoat, brown bear, spotted hyena, arctic hare, arctic lemming, Norway lemming, woolly mammoth (fig. 1.5), giant Irish deer and reindeer all flourished. All are now extinct in Ireland but descendants of these wolves survived until the 18th century.

As the climate cooled about 20,000 years ago these animals would have migrated southwards across what is now the ocean floor to France (the sea level was much lower because a large amount of water was trapped in the enlarged ice-caps). Snow-laden winds from the Atlantic blew across Ireland causing the development of glaciers hundreds of metres thick on the western mountains, in the north and in Galway and Roscommon. Over hundreds of years the ice thickened and flowed under its own weight to cover Clonmacnoise. Polar desert conditions were found in the parts of Ireland not covered by ice and few plants or animals would have survived.

Ice under the pressure of its own weight has strange properties. It will flow like a plastic liquid and the pressure of the ice causes some melting and lubricating as it moves across the landscape. This moving ice is the perfect rock grinding, mixing and compacting agent as it contains an enormous amount of debris.

Such debris may fall onto the ice from surrounding rock faces, fall into crevasses, freeze and stick to the base of the ice, become incorporated in the ice by re-freezing at the base, or it may enter the ice by an important shearing upwards mechanism. The transported rock is crushed and rolled forming a complete mixture of rock types and sizes.

THE LEGACY OF THE ICE AGE : ESKERS

All the low lying hills in Clonmacnoise are eskers, which were formed when the ice

Fig. 1.6
How eskers are formed. When the ice started to melt, each tongue became riddled with a large number of melt-water channels which were like tunnels in the ice (stage A). A huge amount of debris was carried in the water (stage B). Much of the debris consisted of sand and gravel but large boulders could also be transported depending on the speed of the water. The material was eventually redeposited on the sides and the base of the tunnel (stages C and D). After the river stopped flowing and the ice cover had completely melted a ridge of sandy and gravelly material was left behind.

cap was melting, and subglacial streams carried huge amounts of sand, gravel and rocks (fig. 1.6).

LOOKING AT ESKERS IN CLONMACNOISE

All routes to and from Clonmacnoise run along or beside eskers, and these narrow winding roads are often frustrating reminders to motorists that they are following the bed of a sub-glacial stream. Many of the eskers have been quarried or cut and the quarry faces offer an opportunity to examine the varying size of transported material. Care should be taken when examining any quarry face as they are all unstable and permission should be sought from the owner of the quarry.

The majority of the boulders are grey limestone from the local area but it is possible to find numerous other rock types (erratics) that are not local in origin but come from areas to the west from where they have been transported by ice and water — sandstones are particularly common. Erratics were deposited across the surface of the eskers and the surrounding land. Many such boulders can be seen locally, and The Clonfinlough Stone (fig. 1.7), referred to earlier is an erratic.

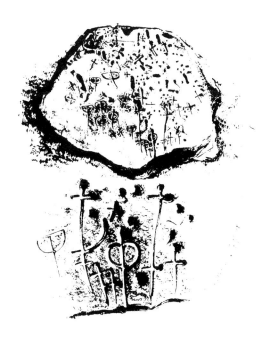

Fig. 1.7
The Clonfinlough Stone is lying in a field near the Roman Catholic church at Clonfinlough. Its unusual carvings were made by Bronze Age Man who modified patterns which had appeared through natural weathering. (du Noyer)

As well as eskers and erratics, fine grained materials or "till" carried by the ice formed a blanket over the landscape disguising the underlying rocks. This is the material from which present day soils are formed.

AFTERMATH OF THE ICE AGE

The ice left behind a bleak landscape where snow could still be seen in sheltered areas. Imagine Clonmacnoise without any vegetation and covered by fresh, crushed grey limestone boulders and gravel. The Shannon, swollen with meltwater from the receding ice mass to the west was probably 20 times its present width and had a grey/blue appearance from the enormous load of ground-up material it was transporting away from the ice. It would have been very cold (well below freezing) most of the year but summer temperatures may have reached 10-15°C.

When the climate began to warm up, the first rain showers in about 10,000 years fell on Clonmacnoise. Water flowed from the eskers carrying fine sand and silt into the low lying areas which eventually formed a thick layer. This was the landscape ready for recolonisation by returning plants and animals.

○
Peter Coxon lectures in the Geography Department of Trinity College, Dublin.

CHAPTER TWO

The Early Impact of Man

Richard Bradshaw

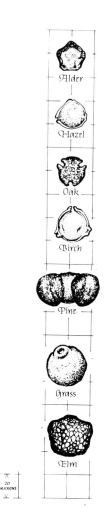

Fig. 2.1
Seven types of pollen commonly found in Irish peat.

INTRODUCTION

Recreating the geological history of Clonmacnoise is comparatively easy as most of the evidence is still to be seen: the eskers, rocks and soils. What of the plants and animals which have lived in the area over the past 13,000 years? There are no written records for almost all of this period yet scientists know that there was woodland in Clonmacnoise 9,000 years ago. They know which plants grew on the bog at that time and even the year the first elm tree arrived.

The study that reveals this information is called palynology and it relies on the painstaking examination of thousands of plant fossils (pollen grains) which have been preserved in peat and mud (fig. 2.1). As Mongan Bog has grown year by year, it has trapped and preserved pollen grains which have fallen or been blown onto the surface of the bog ever since peat started to accumulate. Thousands of years after they have been buried a corer has been pushed into the bog to extract a sample of peat and after examining its buried pollen it has been possible to reconstruct the vegetation that produced it centuries before. As the accumulation of peat in Mongan Bog has been monitored by radiocarbon dating, this allows a precise date to be given to the time the pollen grains were deposited. This technique has been used widely in Ireland since the 1950's and the presence of Mongan Bog has meant that a record of vegetation history has been obtained for the Heritage Zone.

The story which this work has revealed is one of the slow return of plants and animals to Clonmacnoise once the climate improved after the Ice Age, of bogs which were once lakes, of many types of woodland now long extinct, and of the enormous effect of man on the landscape long before the monastic settlement was founded.

THE ERA OF THE GIANT DEER

The story begins 13,000 years ago when the Ice Age lost its grip on Ireland. All the low-lying land around Clonmacnoise was flooded by water but gradually the eskers became covered in a diverse vegetation containing mountain avens, rockrose, juniper, dwarf birch, grasses and sedges similar to parts of the Burren in Co. Clare where many of these arctic-alpine plants flourish today. The rich grazing supported large numbers of Giant Deer with magnificent antlers spanning up to 3.5 m (fig. 2.2). Giant Deer roamed the lowlands with little competition as many other rivals did not return to Ireland after the Ice Age because the journey across shifting sand-bars from south-west Scotland was perilous.

Fig. 2.2
The Giant Deer, ruler of all Ireland over 11,000 years ago.

Between 11,000 and 10,000 years ago the climate again deteriorated. Intense cold broke up the ground and caused land-slides. The lakes were iced over for most of the year. The vegetation thinned drastically and only a few types of plants survived. The Giant Deer which had briefly flourished became extinct as its food supplies dwindled.

This cold period which lasted for a few hundred years, ended 10,000 years ago when the warm period we enjoy today finally began. Water plants and algae started to grow in the lakes and the eskers were again covered in a dense scrub. Lichens, mosses and other plants started to add organic matter to the soil transforming it from bare rock into a fertile substrate for large plants. Willows and birches with their light seeds were the first large trees to appear. Red deer, hares, wolves and brown bears returned to Ireland, but other animals such as the elk, the aurochs (primitive cow) beaver and several smaller animals and weaker swimmers such as the common shrew, voles and mice did not manage the journey, as it was a wet and dangerous crossing. These first animals reached Ireland just ahead of the first hunters.

MONGAN LAKE

Shallow lakes lay between the esker ridges (such as where Mongan Bog is now), and these rapidly filled with marl. Marl is a deposit of calcite (calcium carbonate) which is precipitated out of the water through the growth of algae raising the pH every spring. As the landscape dried out after the ice, and the lakes became shallower, areas of marshy ground were colonised by wetland plants. By 9,200 years ago the open water was covered by a floating mat of vegetation and the lake had been replaced by a fen. Mongan Bog would then look like the fens of the Callow and Fin Lough, (Chapters 6 and 12), with their rich and diverse cover of vegetation. It was a paradise for wildfowl as there were dense beds of reeds, sedges, rushes and willows.

Peat started to accumulate for the first time as the plants growing in the water decomposed only partially. Wherever plants grow in waterlogged conditions, peat will accumulate as the complete decay of plants is prevented. The first peat under Mongan Bog was dark in colour and pollen analysis has shown that it consisted of reeds, sedges, ferns and rushes, plants totally unlike those which now live on the surface of the bog.

THE FIRST WOODLANDS

Fig. 2.3
Remains of cranes found in Ireland show that these birds once danced on Irish peatlands.

Eventually trees such as pine and hazel, which had survived the Ice Age in refuges around the edge of Europe, returned to Ireland. About 9,000 years ago, pine trees fringed Mongan Fen and also grew on the eskers. Only seasonally flooded areas such as the callow were still without any trees. Birds must have come with the pines because in present day pine forests in Europe, one finds a special group of birds including the magnificient turkey-like capercaillie. There were probably crossbills, several finches, woodpeckers and magnificient eagles, buzzards, and owls — many of which are sadly absent today. One of the most exciting and haunting sounds of the great peatlands of northern Scandinavia today is the whoop of the crane — an ungainly but elegant bird which had a long history in Ireland and became extinct possibly as late as the Middle Ages (fig. 2.3).

For a time, pine and hazel reigned supreme, but the speed with which other trees were travelling to Ireland and other types of evidence suggest that the climate at this time was probably warmer and drier than today. Hazel was more common in Ireland than in most other parts of Europe, and may have formed a small tree. Tree-like hazels can still be found today in an exciting remnant of ancient Irish woodland near Tullamore.

How did these forests at Clonmacnoise 9,000 years ago compare with the rest of the country? As a browsing red deer moved north-east into Westmeath, she would have noticed pine disappearing from the drier fertile soils. A trip to the south-west would have brought her to denser pine forests, risking forest fires that may have raged in the warm and dry summers. These woodland areas at Clonmacnoise were unique in European history, and there is nothing quite like them left today.

OTHER TREES IN THE RACE TO CLONMACNOISE

Elm trees were moving towards Clonmacnoise from the south-east at a speed of up to one kilometre per year (fig. 2.4). Oak won the race to Ireland, but they both reached Clonmacnoise at roughly the same time – nearly 7,500 years ago (1,500 years after arriving in Ireland). Elm ousted hazel from the richer soils that hazel had favoured and flourished with hazel on the eskers. Pine survived on the peaty areas with birch and willow. With the arrival of elm and oak, the forest-floor became cool and shady. Our wandering deer was more likely to meet striped boar piglets rooting for truffles, than the wolf packs which were moving westwards to the mountains.

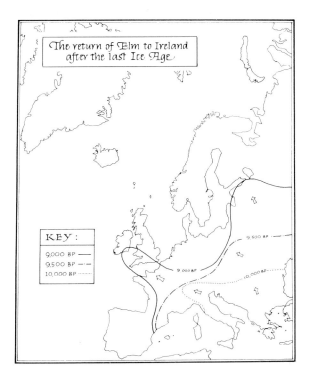

The return of Elm to Ireland after the last Ice Age

KEY:
9,000 BP ——
9,500 BP —·—
10,000 BP ········

Fig. 2.4
The position of the front-line of elms at different times in the past (BP = years before present).

15

THE FIRST HUNTER

This was the landscape viewed by the first man to arrive in Clonmacnoise, the dense, untouched forest, Mongan fen with Fin Lough in similar condition, elm woods on "The Rocks of Clorhane" and swampy forest on the floodplain of the Shannon (fig. 2.5). Almost 70% of the whole country was covered by mixed forest, and the remainder was open water and boggy wetland. Open, heathy, grassy areas were very rare.

Small hunting and fishing parties of Mesolithic or Stone Age man made the occasional foray into the Clonmacnoise area, probably travelling by dug-out canoe and keeping to the banks of the Shannon. They hunted fish and small animals, eating berries and fruits but without disturbing the natural vegetation.

Roughly 6,000 years ago, the climate began to change. Summers were still long and warm, but it became wetter, and alder which likes to grow in wet peaty places started to flourish. Pine numbers fell as alder expanded, and apart from the odd pine and yew, the forests now became completely deciduous.

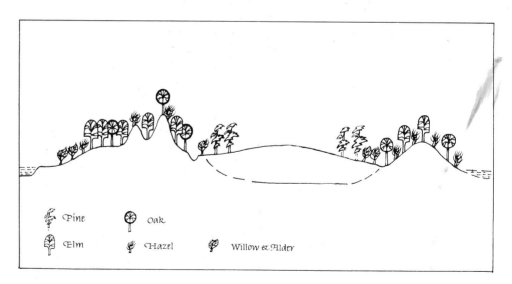

Fig. 2.5
A cross-section from the Shannon to Fin Lough showing the woodland types that would have been seen by the first visitors to Clonmacnoise.

Pine   Oak

Elm   Hazel   Willow & Alder

THE FIRST CLONMACNOISE FARMER

Over the next 3,000 years, man was becoming increasingly active and the paradise

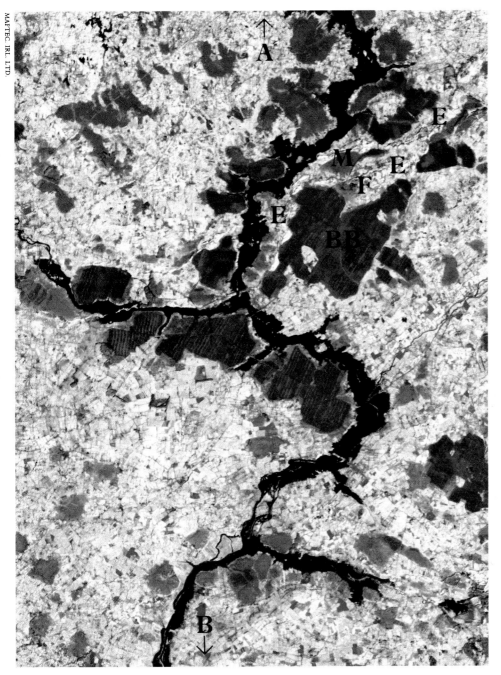

The West Midlands as seen here from a satellite. The area bisected by the flooded River Shannon stretches from just below Athlone (A) to Portumna (B). Most of the landscape features of the Heritage Zone can be distinguished; Mongan Bog (M) surrounded by winding eskers (E), Fin Lough (F) situated north of Blackwater Bog (BB) which is being cut for fuel.

The Pilgrim's Road Esker running north of Mongan Bog was probably part of the Eiscir Riada or Great Road which linked east and west in early Christian Ireland. Its winding shape is a reminder that it was formed in the bed of a river which ran under the ice-cap 15,000-20,000 years ago.

OSCAR MERNE

INGEMAR LEXT

The capercaille was a native of the pine forests which once covered the eskers. This bird has long disappeared from Ireland but it can still be seen in Scotland and in the natural coniferous forests of Scandinavia where this picture was taken.

for wildlife was soon under attack. A more developed culture (Neolithic Man) had arrived in Ireland bringing more sophisticated tools and weapons (fig. 2.6) and which established permanent settlements in many areas based on livestock and tillage farming.

Man began to change the face of the Clonmacnoise area between 5,000 and 4,000 years ago. Forests were cleared to increase the grazing for cattle, sheep and pigs, and in areas with light soil, the first barley and wheat were sown. The development of trade as part of this mixed economy encouraged the spread of many plants and animals and perhaps even disease. The first dramatic decline of elm all over north-western Europe could well have been due to a fungal disease whose rapid dispersal was helped by timber movements. This 'elm decline' has baffled and intrigued scientists for many years. Its simultaneous occurrence at so many sites makes it seem unlikely that selective felling by man could have been the cause, yet man was just beginning to influence the vegetation of large regions. We can only guess at the true cause of a major forest shock that caused soil erosion in many places. The elm decline marks the beginning of the break-up of Offaly's forest cover.

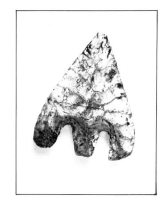

Fig. 2.6
This barbed and tanged arrowhead which probably belonged to a hunter in Clonmacnoise 4000-5000 years ago, was recently found in a local bog.

As people settled they cut further into the forests for timber, fuel and land. Forest composition changed with ash and hazel, favoured by man's activities, expanding onto some of the fertile, well-drained soils that previously held elm. These soils were chosen by man as the most suitable arable land. The Clonfinlough Stone received its mysterious carvings during this period.

THE *SPHAGNUM* TAKEOVER : 3,500 YEARS AGO

Important changes in climate, vegetation and environment occurred as more sophisticated metal-working or Bronze Age people replaced the first farmers. The climate became damp and cool and there was less contrast between seasons. Irish man may have experienced the first of those Irish specialities — the wet, cool summer. These conditions favoured the initiation of raised bog growth and 3,500 years ago the first *Sphagnum* mosses (bog-forming plants) appeared in Mongan fen.

Twelve different types of *Sphagnum* moss have been identified from Mongan Bog, and these plants, dead and alive form the heart of the Irish raised bog. Clumps of *Sphagnum* moss act like sponges, and they can trap and hold water so well that nearly all the weight of a peat bog is rain-water. Puncture this water-filled balloon with a drainage ditch, and water slowly bleeds away. This and other features of the growth of *Sphagnum* (described in more detail in Chapter 8) soon changed the fen into a raised bog, the Sphagnum—dominated habitat which can still be seen in Clonmacnoise.

Peat consisting chiefly of *Sphagnum* moss began to overwhelm trees,engulfing them and invading land on the border of the fen that had been cleared by man for agriculture. The bog also grew upwards and increased in height about 15 cm every 100 years: the golden age of the Irish bog had arrived. This change of vegetation happened in almost all the fens in the vicinity except at Fin Lough, where springs of alkaline water rich in dissolved nutrients kept flooding the fen.

The agricultural effort all around the country suffered from encroaching peat and communications were disrupted. Well trodden tracks across bogs became impassible and the first wooden trackways were built (fig. 2.7). These were used continuously for 3,000 years until modern road-makers chose different routes across the country.

Fig. 2.7
A trackway built across a bog near Bloomhill. Excavation revealed a three-layered structure of brushwood overlain by flagstones and oak piles. The style of horseshoes found on the road helped to date it to the 13th century but the structures beneath may have been earlier.

THE FIRST DEVELOPMENT FARMERS : BRONZE AGE MAN

Despite the climatic set-backs, Bronze age man had heavier ploughs and tools than his predecessors and developed field systems on heavier soils.

His circular houses were set in compounds enclosed by ditches, and a few of his tools, lost in bogs, have turned up in this century. A bronze flat axe found near Clonmacnoise shows that man could beat the forest even if he could not drain the bog, and around 3,000 years ago, the first of the substantial clearances took place on all the drier land. Some of this land had been exploited earlier, but subsequently abandoned in a system of shifting agriculture. Elm, ash, oak and birch were felled, grasses, bracken and other species typical of pastures flourished. Few crops were planted, as cattle-rearing was the main agricultural activity. The find of a ribbon torc gives a suggestion of the cultural sophistication of these cattle-farmers (fig. 2.8).

The fortunes of those early settlers waxed and waned as they were at the mercy of climatic change and marauding bands of rival tribes. Agricultural activity declined somewhat about 2,500 years ago and there was a spurt of growth in Mongan Bog which suggest still wetter, cooler conditions.

When agricultural activity revived again, iron implements were in use during the period called the Iron Age. The forests were attacked with greater ferocity, bringing them almost down to their present impoverished level, with both arable and pastoral farming actively pursued. Only Mongan Bog, Fin Lough and the other major peatlands challenged the total supremacy of man over the landscape and natural vegetation.

Fig. 2.8
This necklet made of twisted gold is one of two gold collars from Clonmacnoise in the National Museum which date from the 4th or 3rd century B.C.

○
Richard Bradshaw lectures in the Botany Department, Trinity College and is a member of the Heritage Zone Study Group.

CHAPTER THREE

Life at the Monastery 1,200 Years Ago

Hilda Parkes

INTRODUCTION

Clonmacnoise is now well known as the site of one of the most famous monasteries in Ireland. It is visited annually by thousands of people, who come to appreciate that period in its history when it was an internationally known institution of learning and piety, an important centre of industry and the place where the most skilled craftsman of the age produced many of Irelands acknowledged artistic masterpieces.

To appreciate the importance of the monastery one can examine some of the works of art created at Clonmacnoise in museums or at the site, the crosses, graveslabs and buildings (fig. 3.1). However these are just a shadow of life in the monastery; to appreciate it fully one must put oneself in the footsteps of the early traveller to the monastery. Before the reader starts on the journey into the past, it is worthwhile to remember what life was like in Clonmacnoise before St. Ciaran's arrival in 547 A.D.

CLONMACNOISE IN EARLY CHRISTIAN TIMES

From the history of the vegetation (see Ch.2) it is known that Clonmacnoise had a settled population before St. Ciaran founded his monastery. People lived within a tribe or tuath and only poets, or other members of the skilled and learned professions, musicians or smiths, travelled freely from one tuath to another. Within these tribes people lived in fixed settlements such as ring forts or crannogs and there were probably several settlements in the Clonmacnoise area. The Bishop's castle may have been

Fig. 3.1
The best view of Clonmacnoise is from the river where the churches and round towers are displayed in the most natural setting.

built on a ring fort and a crannog or man-made island existed at Fin Lough. There were no larger settlements, (i.e. towns) in Ireland at that time such as had been introduced to Britain by the Romans.

Each tribe also had a chieftain who led them in war and peace and was in turn subject to a more powerful chieftain. There was limited trade between tribes whose members' wealth was measured in numbers of cattle and most communications between them took place on the battlefield. The latin alphabet was unknown but a version (called Ogham) adapted for inscriptions on stone had developed mainly in the south and in the west by the 4th century (fig. 3.2).

A road network existed throughout the midlands, graded according to use, from the widest which could take two chariots and had to be maintained by members of the tuatha to the most primitive called bóthar (derived from bó — cow) which were used as cow trails. The widest road called the Eiscir Riada is reputed to have linked the east and west of the country and to have run along eskers in West Offaly (fig. 3.3). The road passed through Clonmacnoise and then turned south along the esker to Shannonbridge where there was a ford over the Shannon. As well as a road network linking the more densely populated areas, there were maritime routes to Britain and Europe. The Irish regularly raided the west coast of Britain which was occupied by

Fig. 3.2
A typical ogham stone, which is interpreted from bottom to top and on this example reads "(the stone of) Maqi-liag, son of Erca".

Fig. 3.3
Almost all the monasteries in the Midlands were near the Great Road or Eiscir Riada which linked east and west and ran along eskers passing through Clonmacnoise.

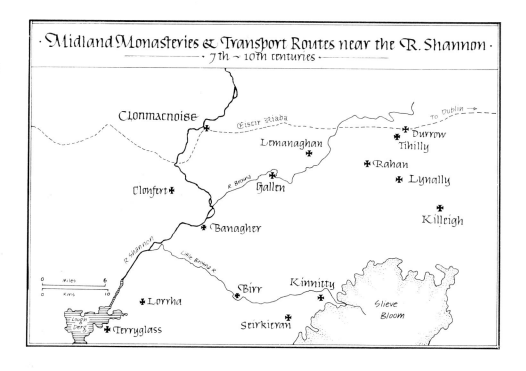

Romans but the Romans were never tempted to retaliate across the Irish Sea which was described by a contemporary writer as that "blowey and restless sea navigable only during a few days in the whole year".

THE MONASTIC TRADITION

Christianity was established in Ireland during the 5th century through the efforts of various missionaries, including St. Patrick who established an episcopal church based on bishops and dioceses. The monastic tradition also arrived at the same time. This had originated in Egypt but had been adopted by Christianity and generally developed alongside the episcopal church wherever Christianity had been introduced.

The monastic way of life was based on seclusion. A monk dedicated himself to a life of prayer and penance taking vows of poverty, chastity and obedience and lived within a community according to a code or rule laid down by its founder. The Irish were particularly attracted to the ascetic way of life perhaps because the organisation was roughly similar to that of the tuath or tribe. It is probable that some monastic style communities under the rule of a spiritual leader were already in existence by the time St. Patrick is thought to have arrived. By the time St. Ciaran was born several had attained international reputations in piety and learning.

ST. CIARAN

It is extremely difficult to obtain factual information on St. Ciaran, the founder of Clonmacnoise. The details of his life were written down hundreds of years after his death and repeatedly embroidered by hagiographers (authors who translated and interpreted the writings of the annalists). It is generally agreed that he was born in nearby Co. Roscommon and studied at several foundations around Ireland before establishing the community at Clonmacnoise (fig. 3.4).

Fig. 3.4
A panel on the Cross of the Scriptures is said to commemorate the foundation of Clonmacnoise by St. Ciaran and Diarmuid, High King of Ireland, who are shown setting the first stake. This image has been adopted as a logo by the Offaly Vocational Education Committee.

There are many reasons why he founded the monastery at this particular spot which now seems remote to modern visitors. The river provided a safe and quick transport and communication route beside the Shannon, yet the monastery is placed high on an esker ridge, far above the winter flood level. The site lies on the Eiscir Riada and is one of the few dry sites which lead to the river. There was good land around Clonmacnoise as it had long been cleared of trees and now supported grassland. Springs produced plenty of fresh water and one of these called Druim Tubrid (the well on the hill) gave the monastic site its first name.

The first community at the site was housed in small huts, placed around a church, the whole being encircled by a low bank or ditch. This ditch indicated the holy area or enclosure where monastic rule prevailed. No trace of the enclosure ditch or huts has ever been found but from evidence found at other sites one can deduce that the latter were small round structures made of wattle and daub (small hazel rods woven together by a kind of underwork and coated in clay). These materials all came from the immediate area (fig. 3.5).

THE FLOWERING OF CLONMACNOISE

Why did Clonmacnoise flourish immediately from its foundation to become in a

Fig. 3.5
A wattle and daub hut had a roof made of straw or sods and walls of willow or hazel.

hundred years an internationally known centre of art, learning and spirituality? It is obvious from hagiography and folklore about him that Ciaran was a particularly inspiring person whose strong personality and teaching greatly influenced and strengthened his followers.

The monastery benefitted from the patronage of strong kings from an early stage which enriched it and protected the community from marauders. In return, kings were buried within the enclosure, a privilege denied to other lay people. As a consequence of its position, at a crossroads in Ireland, communication links were easily maintained within Ireland and abroad so that the monks were kept informed of new skills and ideas.

At the time Clonmacnoise was established in the midlands of Ireland, the Roman Empire which had determined the history of Western Europe was being overthrown by the "Barbarian Hordes". This is the name given to numerous tribes, Vandals, Goths, Elans, Saxons, and bands of ex-slaves who seized power in Europe during the Dark Ages between the 5th and the 9th centuries A.D. The history of the period is dominated by battles, sieges, sackings, as the wealth of the Empire fell into their hands. Art and learning was lost while these separate groups fought each other for supremacy.

England was invaded by the Saxons, Angles and Jutes but Ireland was spared and in contrast to the rest of Europe remained relatively at peace. The monasteries like Clonmacnoise, fostered the learning which had been introduced with Christianity so that as a result Ireland, by the 6th century, was in a position to contribute to the revitalisation of learning and art in western Europe. St. Columba, who had studied with St. Enda of Aran, was one of the most important missionaries to Britain and founded a monastery on the Island of Iona in 563, By the 6th century missionaries had reached Europe and had established foundations in France and Switzerland and as far south as Bobbio in Italy (fig. 3.6).

AN ACCOUNT OF A VISIT TO CLONMACNOISE 1,200 YEARS AGO

[*Note There are no detailed studies on life in Clonmacnoise during the period of this traveller's visit and indeed no specific sources on which to base a reconstruction. This account*

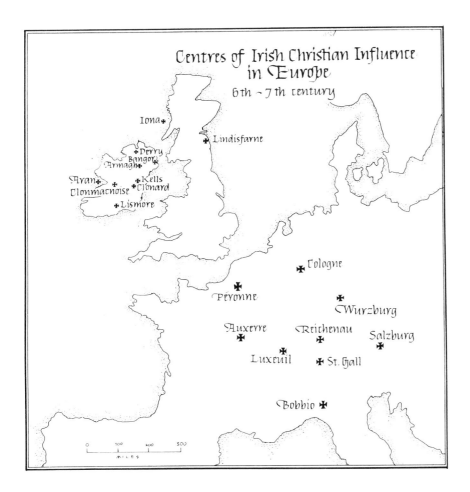

Centres of Irish Christian Influence in Europe
6th – 7th century

Iona
Lindisfarne
Derry
Bangor
Armagh
Aran
Kells
Clonmacnoise
Clonard
Lismore
Cologne
Peronne
Wurzburg
Auxerre
Reichenau
Salzburg
Luxeuil
St. Gall
Bobbio

0 100 200 300
MILES

Fig. 3.6
Ireland was once called the Island of Saints and Scholars from the number of missionaries who founded monasteries in Europe at the end of the Dark Ages.

has been compiled from studies on art and learning in Early Christian Ireland, from the results of research at other sites and work done by antiquarians in Clonmacnoise in the 19th century].

The visitor whose footsteps we will follow for a few days is a French monk who is coming to learn artistic skills to bring back to his own monastery in the Loire Valley. He has sailed from Nantes in a boat belonging to a trader who exports wine, silk, iron-ore and salt to Ireland. They landed on the shores of Galway Bay, the journey having taken a few weeks as the weather was good, sailing in a large currach type craft with keel, mast and sails and rigging. The trader was soon busy negotiating

Fig. 3.7
The figure of a monk carved above the doorway of the Cathedral (11th century) probably differs little in appearance from the monk who greeted the traveller.

Fig. 3.8
The "dairthech" or oak church depicted in the Book of Kells. Under Brehon Laws the costs and specifications of a dairthech were elaborately laid down and a church with a rush roof cost one heifer for every foot in breadth, and foot and a half in length.

a return cargo of wool or hides but then accompanied the student to Clonmacnoise to do business with the monks. The travellers were on horseback and enjoyed free accommodation at all their stopping points as hospitality was just as important to the tuath as to the monasteries.

APPROACHING CLONMACNOISE

As they neared the Shannon they felt they were in a totally strange land as the landscape, dominated by vast brown bogs, was totally unfamiliar to them. Locals must have warned the foreigners about the dangers of bogs and of the necessity of remaining on the tracks high up on the eskers from which they enjoyed panoramic views of this strange bog-dominated land.

Approaching the monastery from high on an esker ridge, they soon noticed signs of its large population. Along the roads were the huts of the Manaig, (lay workers) surrounded by intensively cultivated vegetable gardens. Many currach type dug-out boats could be seen on the river, and from some of them people were fishing with baited lines. A small currach, made from hides stretched over a frame, was being carried over the river bank while the dugouts seemed to be used for the large loads. A dugout boat was rounding a bend in the river from the south. This boat had collected students from Clonfert across the river from Shannonbridge and was landing at the pier below the monastery. Just as the traveller and his companions reached the entrance to the monastery, these students also arrived and there was considerable activity as the guest master appeared to meet the new arrivals.

The traveller noticed that all the monks and lay people he had seen were dressed in a white linen tunic which had a fringe and a woollen cloak which was tied with a pin or brooch. The people working in the fields had tucked up their tunics with a belt (fig. 3.7). Everyone spoke Latin so our traveller had no problems introducing himself. At this stage he bade farewell to his fellow countryman who was taken to a different part of the enclosure reserved for lay people. Soon after his arrival bells started to ring and it was time for prayer.

Since Ciaran's time the church had been replaced several times so that it was now a solid structure made of oak called Dairthech with a roof which seemed to be of thatch (fig. 3.8). The monks and students filed in through a narrow door at the western end but many of the lay people had to remain outside as the church could not accommodate them. The altar was placed at the far end of the church and the whole building was dimly lit by rush lights.

After prayers, led by the abbot, our traveller was directed to the refectory where he had a meal and met other members of the community. They were eager to hear his news and the news of their sister community. Later the traveller delivered a letter of introduction to the Abbott of Clonmacnoise and then he was brought to his cell. He soon fell asleep on a bed made of oak planks after covering himself with some hides.

Over the following few days the traveller was free to explore the monastery and its surroundings and to become familiar with the life and routines followed by the various monks. He was struck by the bustle and activity everywhere. There were monks, clerics, anchorites (hermits living in isolation) and manaigs ruled over by the Abbot, as well as bishops and priests. The enclosure — forbidden to women — was dotted with students, many of whom came from overseas.

Everyone, monk or layman had specific responsibilities in various areas such as the farm, kitchens, schools and workshops just like the monastery in France. There was a fixed daily routine interspersed with prayers and meals and the traveller soon felt at home under the familiar regime.

There were several large buildings within the enclosure which enjoyed pleasant views of the river. As well as the huts and the church there was a refectory and kitchen which were similar in construction to the huts but larger. Near the refectory were washing facilities and the other buildings housed the school and the scriptorium where the scribes worked. All the buildings were made of oak, or wattle and daub. Furniture was also made of oak as well as all other containers, bowls, troughs, plates and drinking vessels.

THE KITCHEN

The traveller first visited the kitchen and storerooms which lay near the refectory. He had a particular interest in the kitchen as he had formerly had responsibility for cooking at his own monastery. He saw how through clever use of an open fire which

Fig. 3.9
The Castlederg Cauldron, which can be seen in the National Museum. A bronze cauldron was every cook's dream in Early Christian Ireland.

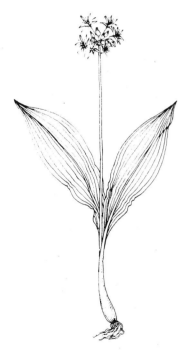

Fig. 3.10
Many wild foods were collected, including garlic, which was sometimes used to flavour butter!

was kept burning all day, fuelled by turf, timber and twigs of gorse and heather, the cook managed to boil, roast or bake food. Water was boiled in cauldrons made of iron or bronze and water for washing was also heated by putting hot stones into cauldrons or wooden tubs (fig. 3.9). Meat was roasted on a spit and bread was baked on a heated flagstone, the forerunner of the griddle. When set, the cake of bread was then propped in a vertical position in a breadstick, a three legged stand with a shelf at the base which prevented the bread from slipping into the fire while it was browned. The standard size loaf served at all meals was two fists in diameter and one fist deep.

After a few days of monastery cooking he quickly realised that the community's diet was based on milk and oatmeal. Porridge made from oats, sometimes barley, was popular hot and cold and was not eaten solely at breakfast but at all meals as a sustaining food. Bread was usually made from oatmeal or barley, rarely wheat.

The storehouses near the kitchen contained stocks of soft cheese and butter (flavoured with wild garlic) which were kept in wooden containers. There were a few boxes containing meat, but it was not eaten often as the monastery could not afford the quantities of salt required to preserve it. The cook knew a little about herbs and flavourings but the visitor was disappointed at the lack of many of the herbs and spices he was familiar with in France (fig. 3.10).

The limited diet was supplemented by produce from an orchard and garden within the enclosure which supplied many vegetables for the kitchen. Among them were leeks, onions, peas, beans, celery, carrots and parsnips. Within the orchard were hives kept by the monks; these supplied the community with honey which was the only source of sugar. A feature of the eating habits of the monastery to which he was accustomed at home was a certain imbalance in food supplies. Autumn was the season of plenty, with fruits and nuts, such as apples, blackberries and hazelnuts. Fish such as salmon and trout were eaten when available. In winter the community would not have fresh milk or cheese and supplies would be rationed. It would be necessary to hunt wild deer, duck and boar (fig. 3.11).

THE FARM

A few days were spent exploring some of the land near Clonmacnoise which was

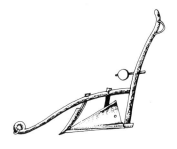

Fig. 3.11
Some of the animals important in the life of the monastery as depicted in the Book of Kells.

farmed by both monks and laymen. The farm satisfied most of the basic needs of the community but not all, as the monks also received rent for land in the form of animals, corn and honey and were regularly given food and materials by rich benefactors.

In contrast to western France, most of the land was in pasture for cows or sheep. Tillage was practised on a smaller scale and while barley and oats were common, only small patches of wheat were sown. In the tilled fields, (through the course of the seasons), fields had to be ploughed, sown, or reaped by sickle (fig. 3.12). Primitive fences were erected around ploughed fields. The corn was ground by simple horizontal mill wheels after drying in a simple kiln (fig. 3.13). Bullocks were trained to pull the plough.

Fig. 3.12
The plough used by the monks was a great improvement on earlier ploughs as it had an iron cutting edge instead of a wooden share and was fitted with a mouldboard which turned the sod.

Farming was well developed in that the monks had introduced more sophisticated ploughing methods and broadened the range of crops and animals kept on the land so that there was considerable local interest in any developments at the monks' farm.

THE LIVESTOCK

From a short acquaintance with the farm it was obvious to the traveller that the most important animal was the cow. Herds were grazed in the most productive pastures and they were always guarded by herdsmen to protect them from wolves and marauders. In summer they grazed on the flood meadows below the monastery but in winter when this land was flooded and fodder became scarce many of the non-breeding animals would be slaughtered. Sheep were kept primarily for their wool and also as a source of milk. Manaig were guarding herds of pigs in the nearby oakwoods as, in a good season, oak mast (acorns) provided them with an important supplementary source of food. Near the monastery there were pens for hens and geese as well as pigs, all of which would be eaten.

Fig. 3.13
This stone was initially part of a hand-operated quern, used to grind wheat, oats and other seeds and was later decorated to become a graveslab.

THE WORKSHOPS

The traveller's main interest lay in the work of the skilled craftsmen — the stone-masons, the metal workers, the illustrators of manuscripts — and his purpose in coming to Clonmacnoise was to learn some of the skills of the manuscript makers. Already it was possible to see evidence of a style and craftsmanship which was to develop and produce in the following centuries beautiful works of art in stone, metal and manuscripts.

The first craftsman visited by our traveller was the stone-mason, the maker of the graveslabs whose work can still be seen in Clonmacnoise (fig. 3.14). The slabs under construction in the stone mason's house were based on the simple design of a cross. The work was being carried out painstakingly by other monks, who had first laid out the designs and were now carving each one.

The Scriptorium was the name given to the building which housed the scribes and makers of manuscripts. Within it the traveller could learn each stage in book production, from the manufacture of vellum to the binding of the completed book. The day he appeared there was great excitement as a book had arrived on loan from a neighbouring monastery and the monks were studying its text. Their principal work, however, lay in copying sacred manuscripts and supplying books for use in the church.

The traveller was greeted eagerly at the Scriptorium as the monks knew he had brought a valuable present to the monastery. The present consisted of the dried eggs of the insect *Kermococcus vermilia*, which the monks used as a dye to produce unusual shades of brown and orange in the manuscripts. This species lives on Kermes oak, and was easily available in France where the particular species of oak grew. By adding alum, the monks could change the colour from reddish violet to purple.

Fig. 3.14
Clonmacnoise is principally famous for its huge collection of graveslabs, which surpasses in diversity and design collections found in other early Christian sites. Many can be seen at Clonmacnoise as well as in the National Museum.

One section of the scriptorum held the raw materials, vellum, inks and quills. The vellum was made from calf skins which were scrupulously examined for imperfections before drying and stretching. He was told that a large manuscript often required the skins of a hundred calves. Other coloured dyes were on display; red, green, and yellow which were made from vegetable extracts and various chemicals. These were kept in containers made of horn near a larger vessel which held the ink. The black ink was constantly being topped up by mixing a mixture of crushed oak gall and sulphate of ammonia. The pens or quills used by the scribes were sharpened regularly by means of a knife (this was the first task given to the new trainee).

One of the monks was cutting designs on bone. It was explained that the illustrations were first cut on bone and this model acted as a guide to the monks involved in reproducing the design on metals (fig. 3.15). Several other monks were examining pages on which the designs were laid out. Different craftsmen worked on each page, either completing the outline of the illustration, colouring the various sections or doing the script.

Fig. 3.15
Part of a rectangular trial-piece in sheep-bone found near Dungarvan (8th-9th century) with familiar motifs. This could have been used as a master mould for clay, silver or gold designs.

The final stage in book preparation required skills of leather workers and metals workers who worked nearby as they consulted with designers of manuscripts in producing protective bindings. Each manuscript had to be given a richly decorated cover and depending on its importance it may have been inlaid with precious stones, gold filigree and enamel. The metal workers were also busy on other projects (other than the bindings for the manuscripts). One was working on a crook of a crozier, another on a container for a relic. Much of this decorative work was extremely intricate and echoed the designs commonly used in the manuscripts (fig. 3.16).

And so we leave this student, busy and content, to spend the following three years in Clonmacnoise before returning to his own community to impart some of the skills he had acquired.

Fig. 3.16
An outstanding example of early Irish art is a bronze mount depicting the Crucifiction of Christ which was found in Clonmacnoise.

The period he spent there was one of peace and prosperity for the monastery and he avoided the plagues, floods, fires or battles which also marked the life of the community. All these events are recorded in the Annals of Clonmacnoise, one of the most important sources of information on early Irish history. The book, known only in translation from the 17th century, may have been written in Clonmacnoise. The Annals record plagues in the 7th and 8th centuries, devastating fires during the same period, raids by neighbouring tribes and frequent battles against neighbouring monasteries! After all these events the monastery managed to recover and prosper.

UNWELCOME VISITORS

Nothing which had gone before could have prepared the monks for the severity of the attacks by the Vikings which started about 790. They had superior seapower

Fig. 3.17
The head of King Sitric, a Viking King of Dublin, is shown on these silver coins. The hoard may have represented "money" to its 11th century owner or it may have been the stock in trade of a silversmith at Clonmacnoise.

Fig. 3.18
The Round Tower provided a look-out with a view over a large area of the Central Plain of Ireland.

○
Hilda Parkes is a research student in the Botany Department, Trinity College, who is studying the history of vegetation in west Offaly.

and weaponry and no respect for the monks, their sacred vessels or books. The first attacks came just as the Golden Age was reaching its climax in the 7th century, and the monastery was attacked at least nine times.

All the blame for plundering Clonmacnoise during these later centuries does not necessarily have to be laid at the door of the Vikings. Local kings who coveted the wealth of the monasteries frequently combined forces with the Vikings, taking advantage of their resources to raid the monastery (fig. 3.17).

From the time of the first wave of attacks there was an increasing preoccupation with security, the round tower was built as a look-out tower and a refuge in times of attack and stone churches began to replace wooden buildings which had been constantly burnt (fig. 3.18). A look-out was always kept to north and south, east and west as the Vikings were known to have a base in Lough Ree but could appear from land as well as from the river. Many of the treasures of the monastery were lost during the raids to appear centuries later during excavations of Viking graves in Scandinavia and Dublin. The manuscripts were useless to a warrior who could not read, but before discarding them, their highly ornamental bindings were torn off and added to his pile of booty, with anything else containing precious metals or stones.

As a result of losing valuable objects, as well as the skilled monks and craftsmen who created them, the standard of workmanship declined in the monastery from the 9th century. The objects and manuscripts of the later period lacked the inspiration and spontaneity of form of previous work, the delicate and intricate patterns were absent as work had to be produced in a hurry to replace materials that were lost or stolen. The influence of the Scandinavians was also felt in a benign way, as the monks adapted some of their designs in their own works of art and copied their boat building technology. After conducting the raids initially from their home bases in Scandinavia, the Vikings eventually settled permanently in Ireland at various ports which gave the country its first urban centres. There was peace for a while as they set about establishing more legitimate businesses. However, new waves of Vikings arrived at the beginning of the 10th century and this led to further battles sometimes in collaboration with native tribes including the well-known Battle of Clontarf in 1014.

The ruins of the monastic settlement of Clonmacnoise. In the background can be seen a large expanse of hay meadows formed by a meander of the Shannon called the Clonmacnoise Callow. This landscape is largely unchanged from that which was viewed by St. Ciaran, the founder of Clonmacnoise in the 6th century.

Clonmacnoise had the status of a city in the 8th-9th centuries. It teemed with monks and various clerics, layworkers, craftsmen and students from Ireland and the Continent.

35

Clonmacnoise was painted several times in the last century by the famous artist and antiquarian George Petrie. A certain amount of artistic licence was used to present the ruins more dramatically.

Among the many treasures from Clonmacnoise is the Clonmacnoise Crozier which protected the wooden staff of a saint.

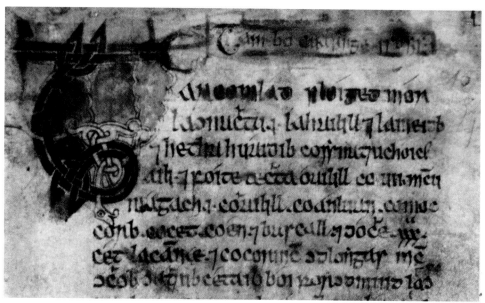

The earliest known manuscript in the Irish language, Lebor na hUidhre, was also written in Clonmacnoise around the 11th century. This page contains the first lines of the Tain Bo Cuailge legend. Anyone with a IR£1 note owns their own copy of part of Lebor na hUidhre, as the manuscript forms an intrinsic part of its design.

CHAPTER FOUR

The Decline of the Monastery and the Emergence of the National Monument

Mary Tubridy

By the late 16th century there was little to be seen but ruins in Clonmacnoise. The bishop had left, there may have been a few monks in the neighbourhood but they relied on the charity of the local people to provide them with shelter and food (fig. 4.1).

This decline in the fortunes of the monastery occurred gradually between 1,200 and 1,500 as Clonmacnoise shared the fate of the monasteries which flourished in early Christian Ireland. However, Clonmacnoise and the midlands remained a centre of learning longer than most other monasteries possibly because it became a centre of scholarship in the Irish language and in the bardic tradition between 1,000 and 1,200.

The reasons for the later decline are very complex and have not been well studied but it is obvious that the arrival of the Normans played only an indirect role in this process. The re-organisation of the Irish church, the decline in the fortunes of its patrons and a general looseness of discipline among the monks all combined to weaken the power and influence of the monastery.

The re-organisation of the Irish church in the 12th century (which occurred before the Norman invasion) reduced the independence of the settlement by establishing for the first time, an effective Diocesan type of organisation in which the Bishop of Clonmacnoise was subject to the See of Armagh.

Fig. 4.1
A drawing by the geologist and antiquarian, Vallency Pratt, of the Nun's Church in the 19th century.

THE ARRIVAL OF THE NORMANS

Initially at least, the Normans were successful in breaking the authority of the Irish chiefs. They also attacked Clonmacnoise and from 1178 the Annals record several raids by Anglo-Norman Lords. As early as 1179, they burnt 105 houses and plundered valuables and cattle. To secure their hold on such a strategic site, a castle was built beside the monastery in 1220 (fig. 4.2).

Fig. 4.2
The Bishop's Castle, near the car-park, was built by a Norman Bishop and was one of a series of castles guarding the Shannon crossings.

Even though Norman power waned in West Offaly after a few years, the Normans had broken the Old Order. They insisted that the bishop and the abbott be appointed by Royal assent and many outsiders, Franciscan and Dominican monks, were appointed Bishops of Clonmacnoise from 1200. The Normans were naturally suspicious of the newly founded houses of regular monks created during the 12th century reforms and supported their own communities; daughter houses of English monasteries.

The power of the High Kings, who had been the benefactors of the monastery had been broken and their place was filled by other local tribes who quickly took advantage of uncertain times. The monastery became more closely aligned with the McCoghlans, the traditional chiefs of the Barony of Garrycastle, who owned the castle at Shannonbridge. This relationship was not always to the advantage of the monastery as the McCoghlans were ambitious and gradually appropriated more and more of the land owned by the monastery. They were particularly successful in managing to steer a narrow course between loyalty to the Norman English and to their fellow Irish chiefs; as a result of their influence West Offaly remained Gaelic much longer than the rest of Leinster. A member of the family called the "Maw" Coghlan maintained the Brehon Laws in Garrycastle until his death in 1790.

There are few records of events in Clonmacnoise between 1200 — 1500 when it must have been surviving in difficult circumstances. While the wealth of the McCoghlans helped to maintain the churches, they also dominated the Episcopal succession and controlled the revenues (fig. 4.3). The last event at Clonmacnoise recorded in the Annals was a raid carried out in 1552 by the English from Athlone. "Not a bell, large or small, an image or an altar, a book or a gem, or even glass in a window, was left which was not carried away," wrote the annalist.

Soon after the raid an Archdeacon was appointed who had authority to obtain a role in the organisation of the community. His imposition was followed by the annexation of the See of Clonmacnoise to Meath (to which it is still attached under Church of Ireland divisions, now called Meath and Kildare) and so from 1568 the revenues of Clonmacnoise were under the control of the Church of Ireland Bishop of Meath. However the offerings from funerals etc. were not sufficient to maintain the new Archdeacon and in 1622 a report on the Diocese of Meath declared the deanery was "wasted and extinct".

Fig. 4.3
This church, called the Cathedral, incorporates portions of buildings dating from the 10th-17th centuries. The 17th century renovations were financed by Charles Coghlan whose contribution is commemorated by a plaque erected on the inside wall.

Fig. 4.4
St. Ciaran's Well is about a kilometre from Clonmacnoise on the Shannonbridge road. Like most "holy wells" it is guarded by a hawthorn or may bush and tradition states that the water has curing properties.

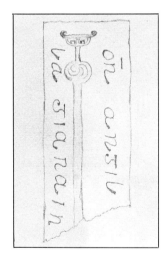

Fig. 4.5
The drawing received from Edward Lhuyd was copied by Molyneux and can be seen among his papers in the Trinity College Library. It must be one of the earliest drawings of a Clonmacnoise graveslab.

This report is also of particular interest as it describes felling in the Great Woods of Clonmacnoise. These were let to O'Malone, whose descendents built Ballinahowen Court, a very impressive 18th century house a few kilometres from Clonmacnoise. The Bishop of Meath was extremely concerned that felling had caused the extinction of the birds to which he was entitled as part of the lease. As well as hawks, falcons and tercels, he enjoyed the revenues from an eel wire on the Shannon, value £3.6s.7d.

The continuity of the Roman Catholic See was maintained with some difficulty after the Reformation and many bishops exerted their authority from Rome. The notorious visit of Cromwell to Ireland in the mid — 17th century brought Clonmacnoise back into the limelight as the Roman Catholic Bishops met there to denounce the tyrant and ask the Catholic population for prayers and efforts to defeat the common enemy, as otherwise all would be deported to the Tobacco Islands.

The Roman Catholic See of Clonmacnoise was eventually joined to Ardagh in the 1750's as it could not support its own Bishop.

While Clonmacnoise no longer had a monastery from the 16th century, the site never lost its religious significance among the local people who kept its history and folklore alive. It continued to be used as a burial ground, but instead of kings and monks, the right to burial was claimed by the local chiefs, the McCoghlans and O'Malones and finally by the ordinary people. Ciaran's feast day was celebrated each year on Pattern Day when people did the "stations" which meant they walked and prayed along a traditional route which included the monastery and St. Ciaran's Well (fig. 4.4).

THE REDISCOVERY OF CLONMACNOISE

Clonmacnoise was eventually discovered by antiquarians in the 18th century following the visit of the artist Blaymire whose views were reproduced in an influential book on the Antiquities of Ireland. There had been few visitors in the previous centuries brave enough to venture into West Offaly which was considered a wild and barren county. Anthony Dopping, the Church of Ireland Bishop of Meath, went to Clonmacnoise in 1684 to see the "Hebrew" inscriptions on stone slabs and later recorded that only two churches still had roofs, St. Ciaran's chapel and Temple Turpan.

Edward Lhuyd the keeper of the Ashmolean Museum, Oxford, came in 1709. He later sent a drawing of a grave slab to his friend, William Molyneux, the Provost of Trinity College, who was a noted scholar and travelled extensively around Ireland in the 18th century but never visited Clonmacnoise (fig. 4.5).

Until the 19th century there was very little serious study on the early history of Ireland. Learned scholars believed that the larger ruins and earthworks were built by the Danes as it was thought the Irish had no tradition of building before the arrival of the Normans. The round towers gave rise to the greatest speculation and among the more fanciful theories postulated were that they were erected for the holy fire of the Druids, or were built by African sea-champions, or were phallic temples. The real significance of the round towers did not emerge until 1833 largely as a result of the research carried out in Clonmacnoise by the famous artist and antiquarian, George Petrie, who first visited the site in 1818 and later called it, "the most interesting place in the British Empire".

A growing awareness of the importance of the site and interest in local history in Victorian times led many visitors to Clonmacnoise. Many arrived by boat as there

Fig. 4.6
A party of visitors to Clonmacnoise in the late 19th century.

was a jetty nearby. It was also a popular picnic spot for the gentry from Athlone, many of whom were pictured in photos in the Lawrence collection, reclining leisurely against the grave slabs while consuming dainty sandwiches (fig. 4.6). Famous visitors included Sir James Ware, Edward Ledwich, Thomas Coote, James Stephens and Samuel Ferguson.

There were regular field trips to Clonmacnoise organised by energetic historical societies. Probably the most successful field trip ever was held in 1886 which attracted 8,000 people and was organised by the Historical and Antiquarian Society. Trains brought people from all over Ireland and the local dignitaries attending the outing included members of the Land League. Interest was fuelled by the current political situation and the newly discovered interest in Ireland's past. They heard a discourse on the history of Clonmacnoise, reflecting the former greatness of the Irish race, and drawing parallels between the tottering state of the Bishop's castle and the contemporary condition of English power and administration in Ireland.

The site remained under the control of the Church of Ireland until 1882 when after Disestablishment, the ruins were vested in the Commissioners of Public Works to be preserved as a National Monument. Temple Conor was excluded as it was in use as a Church of Ireland church.

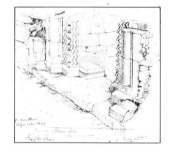

Some maintenance work was carried out at the turn of the century by the State but a voluntary organisation, the Kilkenny Archaeological Society (forerunner of the Royal Society of Antiquaries of Ireland) took the initiative in 1865 by paying for the re-erection of the arch on the Nun's Chapel and other maintenance work (fig. 4.7). A local farmer who kept the key to Temple Conor acted as a part-time caretaker. For a time a hedge school functioned in the cellars of the Black Church which had been modified by the Archaeological Society to be used as a store for the numerous graveslabs which covered the site. Many of the 300 graveslabs which have been found in Clonmacnoise found their way to collections set up by antiquarians, and so finally to the National Museum in Dublin.

Fig. 4.7
This is one of a series of drawings by the antiquarian and artist, du Noyer, of the ruined arch on the Nun's Church. Du Noyer was closely involved with the restoration work carried out by the Kilkenny Archaeological Society.

The site of the national monument remained in the hands of the Church of Ireland until 1955 when it was still in use as a public burial place. In that year the Commissioners of Public Works took over the site and soon started to carry out works to display the graveslabs, and provide facilities for visitors (fig. 4.8). Many headstones were removed to improve the views of the principal features of the site. Early Christian graveslabs were collected from resting places all over Clonmacnoise, many actually buried in graves as it was considered that this guaranteed the custodian a faster passage to Heaven. A display wall was built on the site. This necessitated an archaeological excavation which was carried out by Liam de Paor but except for this type of "rescue archaeology", an archaeological survey has never been carried out in Clonmacnoise.

A highlight in the recent history of Clonmacnoise was the visit of his Holiness, Pope John Paul II, in 1979. This attracted thousands to the area for a short prayer service during a stop-over on his journey from Dublin to Galway. Partly as a result of the publicity generated by the visit, numbers of visitors have doubled since 1981. Facilities for visitors have improved and the Office of Public Works are engaged in a an extensive management programme to ensure the conservation of one of the country's most treasured Early Christian monuments.

Fig. 4.8
The visitors to Clonmacnoise, who now number 35,000 annually, enjoy a feast of early Christian Art. Among the items on display is the Cross of the Scriptures which dates from the 10th century and is so called as it displays events from the life of Christ as well as episodes in the life of the monastery. Rapid weathering in the last 100 years now makes it difficult to read the inscriptions.

○
Mary Tubridy is a research fellow in the Environmental Sciences Unit, Trinity College and is the Project Officer for the Heritage Zone Study Group.

CHAPTER FIVE

The Shannon River

Julian Reynolds

INTRODUCTION

The Shannon is the largest and longest river in Ireland or Britain, rolling its leisurely way for 250 km and discharging nearly 6 cubic kilometres of water each year into the sea. Its tributaries lie in 12 counties and the catchment, which is equivalent to one fifth of the land area of Ireland, has a sparse population of half a million. Throughout the history of man in Ireland the Shannon was a great barrier to trade and tradition, effectively splitting the country in two. Today its broad basin, gentle slope and large lakes have made it a focus for recreation and tourism (fig. 5.1).

SEASONAL WETLANDS AND WILDLIFE

The Shannon and its associated wetlands are home to a rich assemblage of plants, invertebrates and vertebrates, many of which have taken refuge there since the last Ice Age.

After the ice receded and drainage patterns became established in the midlands, the Shannon basin held a maze of shallow lakes and winding channels in a tundra-like setting. The lakes and rivers were invaded by migratory fish such as char, salmon, trout and pollan (lake herring). The bordering fens and bogs were colonised by plants and animals especially those with a northerly distribution today. The recently found Scarce Emerald Damselfly may be a relict species from that period.

Fig. 5.1
The Shannon Basin is low-lying, with many winding tributaries draining lakes, bogs and pastureland.

· The Shannon Basin ·

The flightways of migratory birds, for which the whole Shannon basin is so important, must have quickly become established to take advantage of the vast lonely expanses of open water and abundant feeding and nesting grounds. Many of these large shallow lakes, moulded and sealed by glacial deposits, have over thousands of years become the great red bogs of the midlands on both sides of the Shannon. While once part of the Shannon system, the bogs have their own identity and their vegetation and wildlife are considered in Chapter 8.

The most varied wildlife habitat today is the floodplain of the river (called callow) which amounts to 100,000ha of the Shannon basin. It is particularly wide in the midlands and here it is considered by vegetation scientists to be the richest of its kind in Europe. The seasonal floodwaters swirl over it in winter and the coarse vegetation traps enriching silt and encourages accretion. In summer it dries out enough to allow grazing or hay cutting while its ditches support a rich aquatic and avian life. In winter, the callow is home to thousands of migrating waterfowl. A particularly good example of callow, also unusual in being a communal hay meadow, is found within the Heritage Zone and is described in Chapter 6.

The callow is maintained by the seasonal rise and fall of the river. Despite its size the Shannon flow fluctuates greatly between floods and low waters: at Limerick the measured rate of flow has varied a hundredfold from about 12.4 to 1111 m3 per second, with an average flow of 190 m3 per second. Serious flooding is less common in the summer, not because rainfall is much less but because of higher evapo-transpiration rates from the whole catchment and a greater capacity for waterstorage in bogs, lakes and fens.

In the midlands the chances of flooding are increased by the remarkably shallow gradient of the river. Between Athlone and Portumna the river falls only 12 m over a distance of 40,000 m which means it has a shallower gradient than any other large river in Europe.

FISH

Although the Shannon river wetlands harbour many interesting forms of wildlife such as otter and wild geese, the most sought after creatures in the river are the fish.

Char is apparently now extinct in the Shannon system but many other fish live in its waters which provides some of the best coarse fishing in Europe (see Table 1 for a list of the larger fish found in the river at Clonmacnoise).

Table 1 — Larger Fish Living in the River at Clonmacnoise

Salmon — Formerly up to 25 kg but now extremely rare in the Shannon: licence required for rod fishing.

Trout — Large fish occur but less commonly than in the Shannon lakes.

Pike — Fast growing and long-lived fish eaters; will also take frogs and water birds.

Perch — Maximum size 40 cm and about 1.5 kg; congregate in shoals and feed on small fish, insect larvae and shellfish.

Bream — The commonest coarse fish, deep-bodied, up to 50 cm long and 1-2 kg in weight. Sucks small worms and larvae from the muddy bottom of the river.

Rudd — Very colourful fish, normally 15-30 cm long, which interbreeds with bream or roach to produce hybrids, eats beetles, water-snails, larvae and plants.

Tench — Dark bronze-green fish, lives in slow moving shallow water, rare in Clonmacnoise.

Eels — Migratory species, (females to 90 cm; males to about 40 cm.) which stay in fresh waters for around 20 years, feeding on invertebrates and sometimes small fish. Commercial fishing rights belong to the E.S.B. which operates a weir at Ardnacrusha power station.

Fig. 5.2
Pike, perch and bream are important anglers' fish in the Shannon and its tributaries.

The thousands of anglers do not expect to catch salmon, which are now rare, but trout or some of the many coarse fish which have been introduced to its waters by man (fig. 5.2). The pike was introduced by the Normans in the 12th century and the most recent arrival, the roach, has just moved in from Athlone having entered the Shannon system via the Inny.

A typical catch in the river near Clonmacnoise will include many specimen weight bream, rudd, rudd/bream hybrids and perch. An average angler enjoying this free fishing will catch 100 — 120 lbs. of fish daily. All of the catch will be returned to the river with the exception of eels, pike and sometimes perch which are eaten by gourmets.

The river also holds stocks of freshwater crayfish and many smaller fish species (minnow, stone loach, stickleback, gudgeon, lamprey) as well as pollan, a silvery herring-like relative of the trout found in nearby Lough Ree.

EARLY SETTLEMENTS IN THE SHANNON BASIN

For millenia, the Shannon was a huge empty expanse of wetlands and a safe habitat for all kinds of wildlife. The bogs must have added to the isolating effects of the river, for only where eskers provided an approach to the river could settlements exist.

Early farmers started to clear the drier parts of its borders for pasture and learnt to cope with its changing moods. The river would have been an important transport route between isolated settlements (and an invasion route for marauding Vikings). Specialised river-boats, which are peculiar to the Shannon, soon evolved to transport goods and ferry cattle and people across the river (fig. 5.3).

Flooding has always been a fact of life for Shannonside settlements and the early monasteries were often affected. The Annals document many important floods, including one in A.D. 920 recorded by the Annals of the Four Masters, whose waters reached the Abbey of Clonmacnoise. Twenty-two years later the same happened and half the monastery was demolished by its force.

In the eighteenth century floodwaters extensively damaged Limerick City and other great floods occurred in the 1850's and in 1954-5, the last persisting for four months. Winter floods can last for weeks, isolating houses and farms, and as recently as 1985 and 1986 unseasonal summer floods destroyed hay crops across a wide area. Settlement patterns have always reflected the harsh living conditions; in 1954 a small community abandoned callow land near Clonmacnoise and moved to other farms supplied by the Land Commission.

THE FIRST RIVER CROSSINGS

With changing water levels, the earliest settlers of the Shannon region must have recognised the importance of safe river crossings and landing-places. Before bridges were built in the tenth and eleventh centuries, the river was crossed at fords, which were often impassable in winter.

Fig. 5.3
A type of coracle with a wickerwork frame covered by hide was common on the Shannon.

Fords existed at a number of locations, usually related to gravelly esker ridges which reached or crossed the river bed, such as those at Athlone and Shannonbridge (fig. 5.4). The fords became the sites of strong castles and settlements; at Shannonbridge a castle owned by the McCoghlans guarded the river crossing until the 18th century and its strategic location is shown by the maintenance of a garrison in the Napoleonic fortifications until the 1920's.

Some early crossing points are shown by the presence of toghers or trackways buried under bogs. On the western bank of the Shannon at Clonmacnoise, a trackway recently uncovered at Coolumber leads directly to the river. Today there is a wooden jetty just downstream of the monastic site and we can imagine precursors of it in the same location. In the 19th century there were three jetties within 2 km of the monastery, one at the "Rocks of Clorhane", from which stone from the quarries was transported by boat.

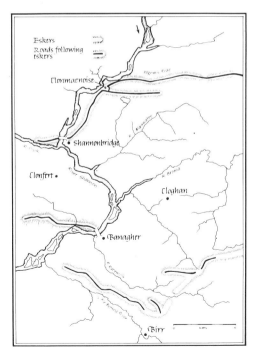

Fig. 5.4
Eskers wind through the bogland, providing early travellers with a dry route to fords and, later, bridges. Today, roads still wind along eskers.

Fig. 5.5
The Napoleonic
Fortifications at
Shannonbridge are unique
in Britain and Ireland.
They were built to guard
the crossing against an
expected French invasion
force but as the French took
a different route they are
still intact.

With the exception of the bridge at Shannonbridge built in 1700 (fig. 5.5) the present day bridges over the river are of recent origin — eleven were rebuilt when the Shannon navigation was improved in 1839-1846 and only in the present century did peat exploitation for electric power lead to bridges at Banagher and Lanesboro.

THE INCREASING IMPACT OF MAN

Despite the low density of people along its banks, human influences have contributed to many changes in the Shannon Basin. The rate of flow was initially affected by the works carried out in the last century to improve navigation. Today its flow is regulated by the E.S.B. to provide water for the Shannon hydro-electric scheme, both at Ardnacrusha and upstream through a series of weirs at Lough Allen, Jamestown, Roosky, Termonbarry, Athlone and Meelick.

Water quality is also changing. Over sixty years ago, a freshwater laboratory established on Lough Derg reported that the lake was unpolluted, its usually clear waters home to a rich variety of microscopic plants and animals and other freshwater life. Fish stocks still included important numbers of large salmon and trout. Today, the lake is more turbid, its mean transparency having decreased and its plankton diversity being reduced; instead there are seasonal "blooms" of algae, which blot out the light attempting to penetrate the water. These changes have been caused by two new elements added to the water in the last 100 years and carried by the river through the Heritage Zone; nutrients from sewage, treated or untreated, from rapidly growing midland towns, and clouds of peat dust from inadequately guarded drains on opencast bog workings.

Sewage enriches the water and leads, up to a point, to more luxuriant plant and algal growth. The peat dust tends to cut down light penetration and where it is deposited (for example, near Meelick and Portumna) tends to blanket and suffocate water-plants, burrowing mayfly, and swan-mussels, and to suffuse clean river-gravels, threatening trout fry and their insect larvae food.

DRAINAGE

Field drainage of the floodplain has been practised for centuries, but a major change in the river's character would take place if the Shannon was subject to arterial drainage. Such a scheme is not new but rears its head after every bad flood and at every election. However, arterial drainage, to be effective, would need to be radical and enormously expensive, and there are strong reasons why it should not be allowed to go ahead.

In purely financial terms, no Irish arterial drainage scheme in the past 25 years has proved cost-effective in terms of added land-value and the soils of much of the Shannon Basin are not outstanding for improvement. Thus, drainage is a social and political option, not an effective means of investment in agriculture.

Drainage would affect the efficiency of the Ardnacrusha hydro-electricity generating station. The Shannon and its lakes are effectively a storage system for the station. The lowering of the river-bed through arterial drainage — expected to be most severe in the stretch between Athlone and Portumna, passing through the Heritage Zone — would necessitate major alterations to the present weirs.

Added to this is the damage to tourism and recreation, currently of prime importance to the Irish midlands. Most Irish drainage schemes have damaged fish stocks and wildlife diversity, and have left piles of spoil and rubble along treeless steep banks, making it difficult or impossible to approach the water, let alone embark or fish. Currently, an estimated 60% of angling tourist revenue is generated within the Shannon system, and this would be jeopardised by drainage. The callow would be transformed to fields permanently above water, losing the diverse fauna and flora and the migratory waterfowl which makes it unique in Western Europe.

THE FUTURE

Fig. 5.6
Increasing numbers of
visitors enjoy cruising
holidays on the Shannon

For two hundred years the river has been navigable from Killaloe to Carrick-on-Shannon but despite canal links with the Shannon Estuary, the Erne, the Barrow and Dublin, it never realised its full commercial potential and water-borne trading finally ceased in 1960. In the past 25 years there has been a transformation in river traffic, with a steady increase in water-borne recreation. There are over 500 cruisers for hire today, and jetties and marinas have been developed at several points along the river (fig. 5.6). These cruising visitors are not quite the usual tourists — many are interested in wildlife, scenery or antiquities; many bring binoculars, and most pack bird-books or field-guides with them, knowing they will have time, tranquility and opportunity for observations.

This group of people — over 20,000 a year, and rapidly increasing — may help to influence the future shape of the Shannon river, its landscapes, fisheries and shoreline amenities. They appreciate the quiet unspoilt stretches of river, with congenial stopping-places, more than the bustle of commercial tourist centres. Any plans to change the Shannon environment will need to bear their special wants in mind or risk losing much of what is most attractive along with the potential revenue generated.

○
Julian Reynolds is a lecturer in biology in Trinity College and is based in the Zoology Department. He is a member of the Heritage Zone Study Group.

CHAPTER SIX

The Callow:
The Original Clonmacnoise

Mary Tubridy

INTRODUCTION

In summer the Shannon is 100 m wide at Clonmacnoise and swimmers frequently cross the river from the jetty as the current is sluggish. With the autumn and winter rains on the midlands the river's breadth increases ten fold. Throughout the Heritage Zone the river's course is no longer visible and the Shannon takes on the appearance of a large lake.

The land submerged during flooding, which can also occur in summer, is called by an Irish word, 'callow'. The flat expanse of land to the north west of the National Monument is a callow and may have given Clonmacnoise its name, as Cluain Mhic Nois, from which it is derived, means "water meadow (cluain or callow) of the sons of Nós". Clon also appears in the names of other townlands in the area, including one immediately north of Clonmacnoise, Clonascra, "water meadow of the scraw" (scraw = rough vegetation).

Callow land offers an opportunity to examine a fascinating community of plants and animals adapted to flood conditions which are remarkably diverse. As the callow was never ploughed or drained, the grasslands are the same as those used by the monks 1000 years ago. While it looks like a large green field, it is divided into roughly 40 small strips owned by different farmers, all of whom manage their land in the same way by taking one cut of hay each year. The meadows provide a rich and varied show of colour and their late cutting for hay ensures that many birds can nest safely on the callow which is alive with birdsong all summer. Because hay-cutting has been the only system of farming practised over the callow for as long as people remember, farming does not seem to threaten the plants and animals and under the present system, farming helps to conserve its wildlife.

CALLOW SOILS

If one takes a soil core on the callow one will find a series of deposits which have been laid down since the end of the last Ice Age when a large lake covered the area (fig. 6.1). To a large extent the development of the callow has followed the same pattern which was described for Mongan Bog (see chapter 2) . A raised bog has not formed probably because the succession has been modified by man who burnt the vegetation and introduced grazing animals.

One of the lower layers consists of shell marl, a fine stickey material containing shells of the animals which once lived in the post-glacial lake. This was used as a source of lime in the 19th century as marl is very rich in calcium carbonate (calcite). Patches are visible on the boundary between the callow and esker soils.

The present soils began to develop after the Shannon's basin contracted and plants invaded its banks. The dense growth of the plants helped to trap silt carried along by the river which encouraged their growth as the rivers silt and clay (alluvium) is enriched with plant mineral nutrients.

Peat then started to be laid down as an indirect result of flooding because the complete decay of plant remains was prevented. Peat formed under the influence of flooding is called fen peat as it is alkaline and mineral rich and one finds a fen type of vegetation growing on this soil. If soil is subject to waterlogging from below but not flooding from above an acid peat develops similar to what is found in bogs. Eventually, through the accumulation of alluvium and the growth of peat, the depth of the soil increased so that the surface was above the water level for a few months each year.

The growth of the various types of peat soils and the deposition of alluvium continues and as there are important differences in elevation across the callow there is an unusual diversity of soils in such a small area.

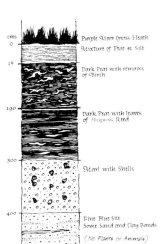

Fig. 6.1
A profile of callow soil.

CALLOW VEGETATION AND WILDLIFE

In the same way that there are different soils on the callow there are also many different plant communities (fig. 6.2). In the wettest areas around the borders of the callow and in the south east corner most plants are growing in water all year round. Starting from the water's edge one finds tall plants such as common reed, our tallest native grass, horsetail and common club-rush which can grow quite happily in two metres of water. The reed was cut for thatch and bedding for animals in the last century. In summer, birds such as coot, mallard, water hens and swans, which one sees on the river, disappear into this reedswamp when disturbed. The water level is always

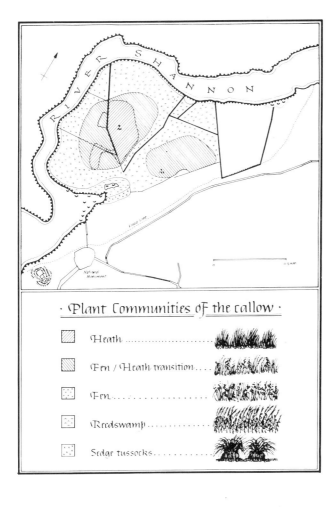

Fig. 6.2
A vegetation map shows the plant communities which have been located on the callow after field studies by the author (assisted by Neil Lockhart).

55

high and so this area can rarely be explored on foot even in mid-summer.

SEDGE TUSSOCKS

Between the reedswamp and the dry land on the esker margin there is an unusual plant community consisting almost entirely of tufted sedge (*Carex elata*), a member of a group of grass-like plants generally found in wet soils. The tussocks formed by the plant are roughly one and a half metres tall (this area is dangerous for those who can't leap at least a metre from tussock to tussock as the soil between them is soft and treacherous!)

HAY MEADOWS

The previous plant communities are not cut at all as they are under water almost all year. Most of the callow is cut for hay (almost 80%) and these hay meadows are found in the central part of the callow where the soil is a mixture or peat and alluvium, the proportions depending on the elevation.

If hay is taken from nearer the river on the west and north , tall sedges make up a higher proportion of the herbage. Farther from the water, one finds a great variety of meadow grasses, as well as broad-leaved plants such as meadowsweet, marsh bedstraw and marsh pea. Marsh pea (fig. 6.3) is protected by law as it is generally rare in flooded meadows in Ireland although it is abundant in the callow.

Many plants contribute to the kaleidoscope of colour visible on the callow; the yellow and purple loosetrifes turn the area just below the National Monument pinky red in early summer. These plants grow about one and a half metres high and among them grow stragglers such as fen bedstraw (*G. uliginosum*) and marsh stitchwort. Ragged robin is abundant in the hay meadows and its tall red waving flower stalk can easily be spotted in early summer followed by the purple lousewort and the common buttercup.

The cattle to which this hay is fed enjoy not only a wide selection of native grasses, sedges and broad-leaved flowering plants, but many of these are particularly high in nutrients such as potassium, calcium and magnesium, as a result of flooding.

Fig. 6.3
The marsh pea is a legume and contributes nitrogen to the soil as it has nitrogen — fixing bacteria in nodules on its roots.

FEN TRANSITION

The highest parts of the meadows, near the centre of the callows, have a distinct vegetation which reflects the infrequency of flooding and so is not as productive as in the previous zone. There are many low-growing sedges with descriptive names such as star sedge, flea sedge (fig. 6.4) as well as bog cotton, sheep's fescue, and the herbs self-heal, red rattle and yellow rattle which indicate a nutrient poor substrate. Mosses grow well here as they can easily compete with the plants.

Unimproved grassland, particularly when it is maintained solely as hay meadow, is of the greatest natural history interest. If this vegetation was grazed, then certain species preferred by animals would disappear and the growth of many others would be affected by trampling or seed removal. In this situation the natural distribution of vegetation types which reveals the past history of the vegetation would be distorted and the value of the whole area greatly diminished.

PURPLE MOOR GRASS HEATH

In contrast the highest land on the callow which experiences least flooding, is not used by farmers. The soil consists of an acid peat, is low in nutrients and so has a limited collection of plants. It cannot be cut as the grass covering 90% of the area, purple moor grass (fig. 6.5), forms dense tussocks which are impossible to penetrate with machinery and it is of little value as feed for animals. Bog moss (*Sphagnum*) forms hummocks in a few places, which suggest that this area may become more like a raised bog if allowed to develop naturally. This is not happening as it is burnt every spring in a mistaken belief that burning will improve the fertility of the soil.

THE CALLOW IN WINTER

As the water level rises it covers increasingly larger areas of callow until at the maximum level the Shannon reaches the edge of the esker ridge to the north of the National Monument, and the only land still visible is occupied by the patch of purple moor grass in the centre of the callow. One can locate the flood margin by following the growth of the black aquatic moss (*Fontinalis*) on stones forming the ditches running from the National Monument to the water's edge.

Star Sedge

Flea Sedge

Fig. 6.4
Sedges such as these can be distinguished from rushes and grasses as they have solid three-angled stems.

Fig. 6.5
Purple moorgrass is almost
worthless to livestock but
the large tussocks which it
forms provide excellent
nesting sites for birds.

Eel Spears

Fig. 6.6
A hunter wading through
the shallow water covering
the callow needed only a
spear like one of these to
capture the abundant eels.

FARMING ON THE CALLOW

Prior to human settlement the callow was covered by swampy forest, dominated by trees such as willows whose remains are found in the fen peat underlying the callow soil. There are still a few scattered willows on the callow but no trace of the original forest remains.

The earliest record of farming is found in the Annals of Clonmacnoise, which refers to the lowland of Ciaran. The annalist states that in the 11th century the callow and 20 cows were given to the poor by Cormac, son of Conn na Bocht. One can assume that the woodland had been cleared from the callow at that time and it was being used for summer cattle grazing.

This was its principal use until the 18th Century and corresponds to the practice of booleying or summer grazing in mountainous areas. The callow was a haven for wild duck and geese which were hunted mainly in winter. Fish such as eels were abundant in the shallow water of the callow and in the last century it was common to catch twelve dozen eels a night. These sold for 10 to 12 shilling a dozen and would have been a source of wealth to anyone who had an eel trap or an eel spear (fig. 6.6).

In an age before drainage and artificial fertilizers, callow land was the most productive in the Heritage Zone and was therefore prized as summer pasture. Even when manuring became part of land management in the 19th century, the callow was still regarded as valuable grazing. The poorest tenants competed for callow land and rents were abnormally high.

At some time in the 18th or early 19th century its use changed from pasture to meadow when the practice of haymaking became widespread and this has been the only system of farming practised in the callow in living memory. In the last century it was the property of two local landlords, one of whom lived in Clonmacnoise House, the large house facing the callow. The land was later acquired by the Irish Land Commission and sold to local farmers and former tenants. Most received 1-acre strips running from the centre of the callows to include hay land of varying quality. No ditches were built on the callow and these strips are delimited either by shallow drains ("lock spits") or in early spring by fertilizer bags. The landowners who own parts of the callow work there for a few days each year fertilizing their strips and saving the hay.

Artificial fertilizer has been applied to the callow since the 1960's, most strips receive fertilizer and it is not known yet what effect this will have on the composition and richness of the vegetation.

Hay is now cut mechanically and it has been possible to cut the fringes of the wet purple moor grass heath zone with the tough blades of the mowing machine. Only the vegetation on the steep slopes ("the levee") around the fringe of the callow is still cut by hand. Hay cutting is carried out in late June, or July depending on the level of the river. In most years a hay crop is saved from the callows but in one year out of 10 the water level rises before the hay is removed and the Shannon denies the farmers the rich harvest.

CHAPTER SEVEN

BIRDS OF CLONMACNOISE

Michael Feehan

INTRODUCTION

Most visitors to Clonmacnoise spend only a short time examining the ruins of the monastic site while on a holiday in the midlands or travelling around the country. Another category of visitor travels in hundreds and spends the entire winter or summer in the area but this visitor feeds on vegetation or insects and views the monastery from 10–30 metres above ground. These are the birds which travel from areas as far away as Greenland and North Africa and which come to Clonmacnoise to feeding grounds which have been in use every year for thousands of years.

The Shannon Valley between Athlone and Portumna is one of the most important bird haunts in Europe and the Clonmacnoise Heritage Zone contains a selection of all the habitats which are used by birds. The river turns into an enormous shallow lake every winter on which one can often see a huge variety of birds (some species in thousands) such as waders, swans and wildfowl. The abundance of natural vegetation elsewhere in fens, esker grassland and woodlands unaffected by agricultural chemicals, ensures abundant food and resting sites and the Heritage Zone, unlike other parts of the Shannon Valley, contains a raised bog which offers a refuge from disturbance.

The winter and summer migrants are probably the most interesting group to the specialist but there are a large number of permanent residents which have been included in the list of almost a hundred different bird species recorded from the Clonmacnoise area (see list at the end of this chapter).

THE CLONMACNOISE CALLOW

The most important site for birds, summer and winter, is the Clonmacnoise callow. In the summer, visitors will find coot, mallard, moorhen and mute swan (fig. 7.1) near the jetty below the national monument feeding on aquatic vegetation, insects, and molluscs; these are only a few of the many birds which breed on the callow. In the hay meadows live meadow pipits, skylarks and corncrakes, the latter easy to identify by its distinctive rasping call which reflects its latin name *Crex crex*. They are now rare in Ireland as the Saharan drought has affected its water feeding grounds in Africa and early grass cutting for silage elsewhere in Ireland disturbs the ground nesting bird.

Fig. 7.1
The mute swan is common all year round in the wetlands of the Heritage Zone. The other swan species, Bewick's, and whooper swans are seen only during the winter.

Possibly the rarest breeder is the pintail duck, which occurs mainly as a winter visitor from Iceland. A pintail was found with five young in the summer of 1984, throughout Ireland it is a rare breeding duck. Also breeding here is the shoveler duck; although not rare, it is a scarce breeding bird in Ireland. The sedge warbler, a summer visitor from Africa, is a common breeding bird confined to the reed beds at the edge of the river.

BREEDING BIRDS OF THE CALLOW

Coot	Confirmed breeding
Corncrake	Probably breeding
Dunnock	Confirmed breeding
Great crested grebe	Probably breeding
Hooded crow	Confirmed breeding
Little grebe	Confirmed breeding
Moorhen	Confirmed breeding
Mute swan	Confirmed breeding
Mallard	Confirmed breeding
Meadow pipit	Confirmed breeding
Pintail	Confirmed breeding
Reed bunting	Confirmed breeding
Sedge warbler	Confirmed breeding
Shoveler	Confirmed breeding
Skylark	Confirmed breeding
Snipe	Confirmed breeding
Teal	Confirmed breeding
Tufted duck	Probably breeding
Water rail	Confirmed breeding
Wren	Confirmed breeding
Whinchat	Confirmed breeding
Willow warbler	Confirmed breeding.

Fig. 7.2
Among the group of birds called waders are lapwings, golden plovers, curlews, godwits, snipes and redshanks. Like the curlew illustrated, they all have long legs and specially adapted beaks for feeding in shallow water.

In winter when the callow becomes flooded the area is populated by numerous ducks, swans, waders and geese. The most abundant species is the wigeon which comes from north-east Europe and Iceland and between 50 – 1500 birds can often be seen feeding on the vegetation. Mallard are less common as they prefer sheltered areas. The tufted duck and pochard can be seen on the water and these can be easily identified by their habit of upending or diving for plants and insects. Other birds such as lapwing and golden plover feed in the shallows as they have long legs and specially adapted beaks for probing the ground for insects (fig. 7.2).

The most important species is the Greenland white-fronted goose (fig. 7.3), which is found between September and March. This goose has a world population of only

Mallard   Greenland white-fronted Goose

Fig. 7.3
The wildfowl of the Heritage Zone include these two species. The Greenland white-fronted goose is protected under Irish and European law. In contrast the law allows shooting of the mallard at certain times of the year as it is a common bird.

WINTERING POPULATION OF THE CALLOW

Species	Maximum Numbers
Bewick's swan	38
Black tailed-godwit	500
Black-headed gull	1,000
Coot	64
Cormorant	6
Curlew	220
Dunlin	46
Golden plover	900
Greenshank	1
Grey heron	2
Great crested grebe	2
Great black-backed gull	2
Greenland white-fronted goose	90
Herring gull	2
Hen harrier	1
Jack snipe	1
Lapwing	1,000
Little Grebe	2
Mallard	52
Moorhen	6
Mute swan	56
Pochard	102
Pintail	86
Redshank	22
Shoveler	68
Shelduck	2
Snipe	72
Teal	320
Tufted duck	106
Wigeon	1,500
Whooper swan	92

18-20,000 birds and three quarters of them overwinter in Ireland. While most birds who come to Ireland stay near the Wexford slobs small groups overwinter in bogs and wetlands. The flock which feeds on grasses in the callow moves between Athlone and Portumna each winter, using various areas, particularly the Little Brosna callow as well as the Clonmacnoise callow. In the shooting season numbers are low, in the region of 20 – 30 birds, but in spring this rises to 90.

FIN LOUGH

Arriving at Fin Lough in Spring one is immediately aware of a large noisy colony (600 birds) of black-headed gulls which nest on an island in the lake. These birds which are associated with the coast were formerly very common on raised bogs and it is likely that the Fin Lough colony originally nested on the large Blackwater Bog to the south which has now been cut.

It can be frightening to walk here during the breeding season. The gulls are very aggressive during this time and as you walk along the edge of the lake winged bombers descend to within inches of your head. This is certainly the largest colony in the midlands; and from it, birds can be seen foraging for food in fields within a 10 kilometre radius.

Fin Lough is important for many other breeding birds. An unusual, rare breeding bird is the grasshopper warbler which nests among the reeds and feeds on insects and their larvae. It is rarely seen and is usually identified by its song which resembles the sound of a grasshopper clicking its legs. The grasshopper warbler is a summer visitor from Africa; therefore, a breeding pair is very unusual.

The ringed plover is usually found near coasts but they do occur on some of the inland lakes during the breeding season. The ringed plover nests along the edge of Fin Lough near the railway tracks. It is an extremely difficult nest to find as the eggs blend in with the surroundings and the bird has a habit of trying to distract you away from the nesting area by pretending to have an injured wing.

Fig. 7.4
Snipe (also waders) are common around Fin Lough and on the callow. When disturbed, a snipe explodes into the air, flying in a zig-zag pattern and uttering a distinctive rasping call.

Other birds nesting here include the mute swan, coot, water rail, whinchat, stonechat and snipe (fig. 7.4). Mute swan can be seen all year but mainly during the winter when numbers reach fifty. As a winter sanctuary, it is not of great importance compared to the callow. Small numbers of wigeon, teal, mallard and tufted duck occur. As the lake is easily accessible to hunters, one of whom has a boat, the birds are constantly disturbed during the hunting season.

BIRDS OF FIN LOUGH

Black-headed gull	R. B.
Coot	R. B.
Dunnock	R. B.
Grey heron	R. N/B.
Grasshopper warbler	S/V B.
Hooded crow	R. B.
Jack snipe	W/V N/B.
Little grebe	R. B.
Mallard	R. B.
Moorhen	R. B.
Mute swan	R. B.
Reed bunting	R. B.
Ringed plover	S/V B.
Snipe	R. P.
Stonechat	R. B.
Tufted duck	R. P.
Teal	R. B.
Water rail	R. B.
Willow warbler	W/V N/B.
Wigeon	W/V N/B.
Wren	R. B.

R = Resident
B = Confirmed breeding
P = Probably breeding
N/B = Not breeding
W/V = Winter visitor
S/V = Summer visitor

Fig. 7.5
This small bird (11 cm), a willow warbler, is the commonest warbler species and in size, shape and colour looks like a leaf.

○
Michael Feehan is a wildlife ranger from Birr who works for the Forest and Wildlife Service.

"THE ROCKS OF CLORHANE"

The hedgerows and woods at Clorhane provide suitable cover for a good number of smaller birds. In Clorhane Wood one finds summer visiting warblers: the blackcap, the willow warbler (fig. 7.5), the chiffchaff, and the whitethroat. Another bird which is attracted to rocky areas and seems at home on the limestone area at Clorhane is the wheatear which comes from Africa in summer. In all, over thirty species of bird nest in this area.

The yellow hammer is almost confined to roadside hedgerows at Clonmacnoise. It appears to be commonest in the area immediately east from Fin Lough. The sand martin is also catered for in this area, as the quarried eskers provide suitable nesting sites.

MONGAN BOG

Mongan is principally important as a refuge area for Greenland white-fronted geese. There are other species of bird on Mongan (fig. 7.6), but one which has been lost in the past couple of years is the red grouse. A good number of snipe can be found on the bog mainly in winter and curlew use the bog in lesser numbers. The cutaway area at the edge provides habitat for herons, reed bunting, whitethroat, wren and stonechat among others.

CHECK-LIST OF BIRDS OF CLONMACNOISE

Blackbird, Blackcap, Brambling, Bullfinch, Barn owl, Black-tailed godwit, Black-headed gull, Bewick'swan, Blue tit

Chiffchaff, Coot, Cormorant, Corncrake, Cuckoo, Curlew, Collared dove, Common sandpiper, Common snipe, Coal tit

Dipper, Dunlin, Dunnock

Fieldfare

Goldcrest, Goldfinch, Greenland white-fronted goose, Greenfinch, Greenshank, Great crested grebe, Grey heron, Golden plover, Great black-backed gull, Great tit, Grey wagtail, Grasshopper warbler

Hooded crow, Herring gull, Hen harrier

Jackdaw, Jacksnipe

Kestrel, Kingfisher

Little grebe, Lapwing, Linnet, Long-eared owl, Long-tailed tit

Magpie, Mallard, Merlin, Moorhen, Meadow pipit, Mute swan, Mistle thrush

Nightjar

Pochard, Pied wagtail

Redpoll, Redshank, Redwing, Robin, Rook, Reed bunting, Red grouse, Ringed plover, Raven

Stock dove, Sand martin, Short-eared owl, Shelduck, Shoveler, Siskin, Skylark, Sparrowhawk, Starling, Swift, Song thrush, Sedge warbler, Stonechat, Swallow, Spotted flycatcher

Tufted duck, Teal, Treecreeper

Wood pigeon, Whitethroat, Willow warbler, Wren, Wigeon, Wheatear, Woodcock, Whinchat, Whooper swan

Yellow hammer

Fig 7.6
Most turfcutters associate their tough task with the song of the skylark, uttered from a tiny fluttering form high in the air. Like the meadow pipit, it is a common resident of bogs and open ground.

CHAPTER EIGHT

The Story of Mongan Bog

Mary Tubridy

INTRODUCTION

The first people to come to Clonmacnoise saw the land even before bogs formed, when fens covered the low lying areas and it was possible to see the base of the esker ridges.

By the time the monastery was established, the domes of the raised bogs were growing over the fens and peat was creeping up the sides of the eskers. Travellers on the "Pilgrims Road" would have seen a vast extent of peatland below them stretching to the horizon. Pilgrims from the continent must have been amazed by this sight as nothing similar would have been found elsewhere in western Europe.

Of the bogs in the area, only one now remains virtually intact: Mongan Bog, situated 1 km east of the monastery (fig. 8.1). The other bogs were intact until the 1960s when exploitation for turf led to their drainage and removal. Their story is told in Chapter 9. (A newly wedded David Bellamy, who came to Clonmacnoise before large scale exploitation started, later declared it was the most exciting event of his honeymooon!). The preservation of Mongan Bog makes the area extremely special to scientists as these bogs are now almost extinct. Increasing numbers are visiting the area to study the bog which is being conserved by An Taisce.

Because Mongan is still intact, it provides a tangible link with the past as its appearance now is little changed from the time of the monastic settlement. Its story provides an account of an unusual and important habitat which has had a great influence on the landscape and on life in Clonmacnoise since earliest times.

THE BOG THREE THOUSAND YEARS AGO

The bog was originally surrounded by a fringe of wetland called a "lagg", into which surplus water drained from the bog and the esker ridges. It would have been difficult

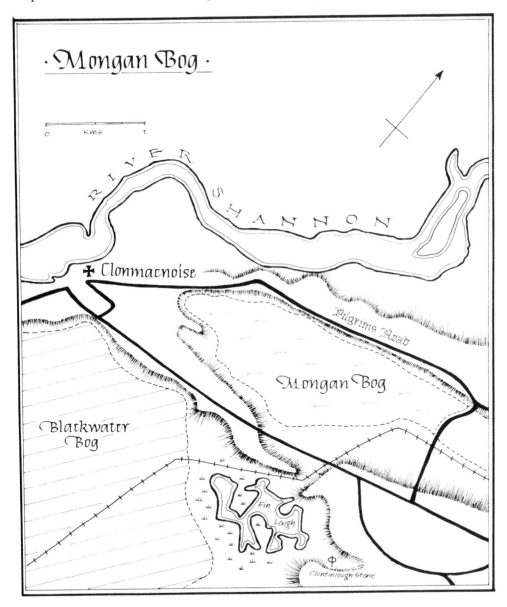

Fig. 8.1
Mongan Bog is one of the few raised bogs left in Western Europe. Its conservation by An Taisce makes Clonmacnoise extremely special to scientists and to the growing number of people who want to learn about the unique features of bogland.

to penetrate at all times as the vegetation in the lagg consisted of a tangled mass of trees (willows and birches) in a soft peaty soil. The lagg included an area of open water which increased in extent in winter, and a rich fen vegetation would have been found fringing it, similar to present-day fens found in Fin Lough and the callow. This area may have been important for the earliest hunters as ducks and geese were abundant in winter.

The presence of the lagg meant that the edge of the bog (called the "rand") was also wet but because the rand was on a slope, nutrient-rich water and oxygen flowed down its sides allowing a wide variety of plants to grow. Therefore, before the arrival of man the pristine bog ecosystem consisted of two areas; 1) a dome of water saturated peat; and 2) a fringe of wetland. These depended on each other, as water from the bog fed the wetland fringe and the presence of this wetland helped to maintain the saturated conditions around the margin of the bog (fig. 8.2).

However, no trace now remains of the original lagg or rand on the bog or on any other large raised bog in Ireland. The area now called Mongan Bog consists of the remaining dome of water-saturated peat. This has retained most of the characteristics of the habitat which started to form nine thousand years ago and which would have been seen by the first intrepid explorers able to cross the lagg. Three thousand years later it can still be seen in the same condition but with far less effort by the modern visitor.

WHAT THE PRESENT DAY EXPLORER CAN SEE

While the bog surface appears flat and featureless from a distance (the best view is still from the Pilgrim's Road), close inspection reveals an irregular terrain in which

Fig. 8.2
A cross-section of a raised bog with an intact margin.

Dome

Lagg Rand

Rand Lagg

When the Shannon floods, the surrounding countryside turns into a vast shallow lake. This flooding has resulted in the creation of a habitat which is of international importance for wildlife, plants and birds.

Colourful pastures are also found on the esker ridges where the variety in plant life is matched by a diversity of insects. The Small Tortoiseshell, which is seen here pollinating field scabious, is a common butterfly in the esker pastures and meadows.

Flooded areas dry out in summer and provide valuable summer grazing and hay. Among the colourful hay meadows on the Clonmacnoise Callow one can still find the shy corncrake.

69

The pochard which winter on the Shannon callows come from either Britain or the Continent. They are excellent divers and obtain all their food, such as small animals and plants, by diving under the water.

The redshank is easily identified by its distinctive organge-red legs. It is a wader which feeds mostly on earthworms and the larvae of flies and beetles.

Almost three quarters of the world's population of Greenland White-fronted Geese fly here every year to overwinter in Ireland's wetlands.

70

there are patches of varying wetness and an abundance of open water pools. Strange as it might seem, the bog gets wetter as one climbs higher above the surrounding land.

The driest and safest areas are called hummocks (fig. 8.3) and, while they are dotted throughout the bog, they become larger the farther away one moves from the edge. Some of the hummocks are 150 cm high and hold the midlands record for raised bog hummocks.

The following plants will probably be found on all reasonably sized hummocks: ling heather, cross-leaved heath, bog rosemary, bog cranberry, bog cotton; and, less commonly, round-leaved sundew and bog asphodel.

Both ling heather and cross-leaved heath form low bushes and can be distinguished by the arrangement of their leaves (fig. 8.4).

The heathers are members of the plant family Ericaceae. Nearly all members of this family prefer acid soils (which is why gardeners need peat beds for heathers if their garden soil is not acid). However, heathers have to struggle to cope with the wet acid conditions of the bog. A plant twenty years old may have a stem diameter of only a few centimetres.

As ling heather is common in dry areas it supplies food and shelter to many animals and even other plants. Epiphytic lichens clothe the oldest stems and grow as luxuriantly in the humid microclimate of the bog as on trees. Many small flies and moths will

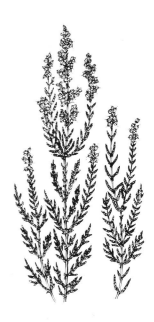

Fig. 8.4
The most abundant heather is ling heather which has leaves tightly pressed to the stem. Cross-leaved heath, as its name suggests, produces leaves which radiate from the stem.

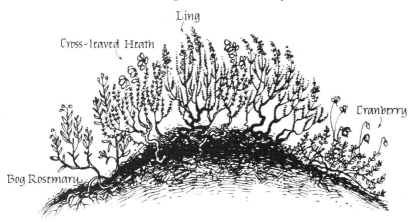

Ling

Cross-leaved Heath

Cranberry

Bog Rosemary

Fig. 8.3
As the hummocks are the driest areas on the bog, heathers grow particularly well on them together with some rare plants which are found only on raised bogs.

71

Fig. 8.5
The largest herbivore living on the bog is the hare, which eats bog-cotton, deer sedge and sometimes heather.

emerge from its branches if disturbed but they are simply using the plant as a safe perch. The leaves are protected from direct attack by insects as they have a tough outer layer. Insects such as leaf miners can bore under this resinous outer layer to get at the soft plant tissue underneath, while others with piercing mouthparts suck the sap.

Hares and grouse eat soft shoots produced in spring. Grouse have not been seen on Mongan Bog for several years but it is very common to disturb hares (fig. 8.5) on or near hummocks as they build their forms on the drier peat. Once sighted, they shoot across the bog deftly avoiding pools, sending up splashes of water from well-worn trails.

"LAWNS" — THE SUCCESS OF *SPHAGNUM*

The relatively flat areas are called lawns and make up most of the bog surface. Within the lawns, one finds the most important bog-forming plants, *Sphagnum* spp. or bog mosses (fig. 8.6). As peat consists principally of the remains of this plant, it means that the growth of *Sphagnum* is of paramount importance to the survival and growth of the bog.

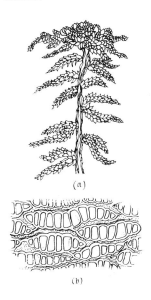

(a)

(b)

Fig. 8.6
Most Sphagnum plants have long thin stems like those shown in (A) and leaves (B) which if examined under the microscope are seen to have a large number of dead cells whose function is to store water.

All mosses have certain characteristics which allow them to flourish in poor soils with fluctuating water supplies. They do not have roots but instead can absorb nutrients through all their parts, including leaves and stems, which is particularly useful on a bog where all the nutrients arrive in the rainfall. As the leaves are almost transparently thin, oxygen (always in short supply in waterlogged soils) can diffuse easily into the leaves. As well as these adaptations, *Sphagnum* possesses two others which have guaranteed its supremacy in bogs.

The plants have large dead cells alternating with live ones (see fig. 8.6b). The dead cells are perforated allowing them to soak up large amounts of water so that the plant behaves like a vast sponge. As one's foot sinks into the soft green carpet of moss, it is easy to believe that each plant holds 25 times its own weight in water. This supply of water guarantees adequate moisture and nutrients for the leaves but makes life extremely difficult for other plants.

The bog "soil" is extremely acid, sometimes with a pH as low as 3, because of the growth of *Sphagnum*. As the moss grows, it absorbs selectively plant nutrients in the form of ions but also releases hydrogen ions, thus causing the low pH. The acidity thus produced creates a bog soil which is the most naturally acid soil in Ireland.

There are various species of *Sphagnum* on the bog which are adapted to growth in the different habitats and whose pattern of growth has resulted in small scale differences in topography on the surface of the bog. On the driest areas are found the hummock-forming species which grow initially in the form of a rounded tussock. This gradually grows higher and wider so that a conspicuous hummock develops and if a hummock is unburnt it will continue growing for hundreds of years. As this hummock is now drier than the flatter lawn, other plants described in the previous section colonise its surface.

In contrast to the hummock-formers, the *Sphagnum* spp. growing on the flatter areas grow more loosely and never form hummocks.

OTHER PLANTS ON THE "LAWN"

While *Sphagnum* mosses form the most conspicuous type of vegetation, other plants are also found. These include, bog asphodel (fig. 8.7), bog cotton (two types: one has a single flower-head and the other has several flower-heads on each stem), deer sedge, carnation sedge, ling heather, cross-leaved heath and lichens.

Some of these plants are confined to bogs but all grow on the bog only because they possess important adaptations which enable them to tolerate the wetness and lack of nutrients. The first three have air spaces in their roots. The plants are perennials, which is a growth habit suited to habitats of low nutrient status, and the new roots they produce each year are formed in the uppermost layers of peat to take advantage of the meagre oxygen and nutrient supplies.

The commonest lichen species on Mongan is *Cladonia portentosa*. A lichen is an unusual plant as it is formed by an association between a fungus and an alga. This takes various shapes, but most people are familiar with the crustose type found on old gravestones. *Cladonia portentosa* is a fruticose lichen and grows as a pale green netting

Fig. 8.7
The bog asphodel is also called brittle-bones, either because of the brittle appearance of its stems when dry or because it was blamed for the weak bones in sheep which grazed on bogs. Either explanation is plausible.

73

over plants in the lawn. It is soft and spongy when wet and crispy when dry.

The most important groups of animals on the flat surface of the bog are insects and spiders, particularly spiders which feed on flies and moths, many of which are probably blown onto the bog from the land on the margin. Spiders compete with each other and with ground beetles and water bugs for their meals. While spiders are watching for their rivals, they may also provide a meal for frogs which prey on them. Bogs are particularly suitable habitats for frogs (fig. 8.8) as pools provide breeding grounds for tadpoles and the adult frog can range in safety over the bog.

Fig. 8.8
The frog is the only reptile found on Mongan.

POOLS: TRAPS FOR THE UNWARY EXPLORER

The most remarkable physical feature of a bog is the presence on its surface of a pattern of permanent pools which have always made bog exploration a risky business. While they vary in depth, many are deeper than the explorer is tall and should always be treated with caution.

It is in and around the large permanent pools that one finds insectivorous plants, that unusual group of plants which manages to get its own back on the animal kingdom (most of whose members live by devouring plant material of one kind or another). In Ireland, insectivorous plants are largely confined to bogs and there are three species on the bog surface; two species of sundew, a round leaved type on hummocks and a long leaved type at the margin of pools; the third species is bladderwort.

The long leaved sundew (fig. 8.9) is easily identified fringing permanent pools as each of the leaves is covered by up to 200 sticky tentacles to trap the insects which happen to alight on them. The body of the hapless victim then decomposes on the leaf, hastened by digestive enzymes produced by the plant.

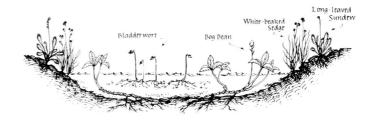

Fig. 8.9
The plant community in a typical pool includes two species of insectivorous plants.

Bladderwort is an aquatic, insectivorous plant (fig. 8.10) which uses a different strategy for trapping insects. It is relatively inconspicuous with a narrow stem and finely divided leaves but some of the leaflets are modified to form tiny bladders. These are normally filled with air and at the entrance there is a trap door. If this is brushed by a small insect the door opens and water and insect is "whooshed" in. There is no escape and the insect eventually dies in solitary confinement in the chamber.

These unusual adaptations offer this group of plants a means of augmenting supplies of minerals such as nitrogen and phosphorus which are in short supply in bogs.

Other plants to be seen around pools include bog bean, beaked sedge and *Sphagnum* species.

Beaked sedge forms a light green fringe to pools in summer. It is a grass-like plant with narrow leaves and inconspicuous whitish flower-heads. In winter this plant provides an important food for Greenland white-fronted geese which sometimes feed on the bog. At that stage the nutrients of the plant are stored in a small bulb at the base of the plant which the geese dig out with their webbed feet. They provide a high-calorie protein and mineral rich food but as they are very small a great deal of foraging is needed to supply a square meal.

Besides copepods (fig. 8.11) (tiny microscopic animals continually at risk from innocent-looking bladderworts) many large aquatic insects can be seen in the pools, particularly those floored with *Sphagnum*. These include small beetles, mites and dragonfly larvae. Many of these are also carnivorous and rely on insects falling into the pools from surrounding vegetation. The most successful carnivore on the bog is the dragonfly (fig. 8.12), which can be seen hawking over pools in mid-summer. Each permanent pool probably has a dragonfly which hovers over the water, watching for prey with enormous eyes and ready to chase off any dragonfly rival in its territory.

THE PAST 3000 YEARS: THE IMPACT OF MAN ON THE MARGIN OF MONGAN

Man was attracted to bogs by the wildlife which was abundant in the surrounding wetlands. Cutting and clearance of the timber was later carried out by Neolithic men,

Fig. 8.10
Bladderwort and sundew will be seen on the bog during spring and summer as they are perennials and die back in winter. The bladderwort has a pale yellow flower which is found in May and June raised on a long spike above the water.

Fig. 8.11
A tiny copepod, barely visible to the naked eye, is a favourite food of the bladderwort plant.

Fig. 8.12
The adult stage of the dragonfly survives for a few weeks on the bog. These insects are particularly well adapted for hunting as they have powerful jaws and can catch prey in flight with the hairy bristles on their legs.

who removed willows and birches. They also cultivated land but initially probably concentrated their efforts on drier ground on the margins of the eskers.

While the lagg soil was very wet, it consisted of fen peat and was actually one of the most fertile soils in the area. The early farmers may have realised that, if adequately drained, it would provide a bumper crop from its cultivation and good grazing in summer.

The soils which farmers cultivate in the original lagg are called peaty gleys (fig. 8.13) and, as they are subject to waterlogging, adequate drainage is still essential to maximise their potential. Even though the original peat was alkaline, they now need regular

Fig. 8.13
Rough grassland which was reclaimed from around the margin of Mongan Bog.

Fig. 8.14
One of the commonest plants of wet meadows is the meadowsweet which likes a limey soil.

liming as rainfall continually leaches calcium from the soil. The presence of rushes is an indicator of this type of pasture and where fields have not been reseeded, the vegetation is a rich mixture of native grasses and herbs including Yorkshire fog, white clover, sorrel and meadowsweet (fig. 8.14).

During early clearances of the natural vegetation, the bog probably experienced its first fires as burning was frequently used as a tool to clear rough vegetation. Fires may have removed the plants on the bog and caused it to dry out slightly but ash blown in from fires in the surrounding areas could have fertilised its surface by bringing in phosphorus and potassium.

Did the monks at Clonmacnoise cut turf? Perhaps they did as turf was used in pre-

Christian Ireland. This was the only fuel available after trees had been cleared in the 17th century, but probably for centuries before that Mongan was cut for turf. Hand cutting for turf has left a legacy of high facebanks all around Mongan on which one can still see the marks of the "slean", the hand cutting tool used to cut the peat (fig. 8.15).

The peat taken from the edge and the base of the bog, fen peat, is highly regarded as a fuel. It burns better, longer and hotter than peat from the dome of the bog because it contains the remains of woody plants which grew in the fen and so for that reason was known as stone turf in Westmeath in the 17th century.

Fig. 8.15
Notice the clean edge around the margin of Mongan resulting from the work of turf-cutters whose sléans have been eating into the peat for hundreds of years.

OTHER PAST USES OF THE BOG

As well as turf the bog was a source of marl which was dug out from below the fen peat. Burnt "scraw" (bog vegetation) and peat ash were used as fertilizers in the last century when it was common practise to mix them with manure on land cultivated for potatoes.

The bog also supplied timber, usually fossil pine stumps which had been buried by layers of peat. Some are exposed on the south margin of Mongan between the road and the bog. The bog pools were used as retting ponds for flax grown in the late 18th century. This was commonly cultivated in the Barony of Garrycastle in which Mongan is situated. The acidity of the water caused the plant tissues to decompose and released the flax fibres. Turf-cutters have found old bundles of flax buried below the surface of the bog and in places where pools no longer exist.

BOG INTO FIELDS: THE PAST 300 YEARS

Because of the enormous pressures on land in the 18th and 19th centuries and the abundance of labour, cutting away of the peat for turf was followed by reclamation (fig. 8.16). Once a sufficiently large area was cut away, the drains inserted by turf-cutters were deepened and a new field created. The soil was fertilised by burning a few inches of peat, and limed by spreading marl (from the Shannon or Fin Lough) or gravel on the surface. These fields were then used to grow potatoes or sometimes rye and when exhausted, they lay fallow for a few years.

In some situations, fields were also created on the bog surface by the poorest classes who were allowed to develop the bog rent-free for a few years. They built sod houses of turf and if successful in reclaiming the bog surface, rent was then levied by the landlord. Several of these fields, called "bog gardens", can be seen around Mongan (fig. 8.17). They would have required enormous inputs of fertilizer and lime as well as labour and without intensive management many later reverted to bog.

All "bog gardens" were used originally to grow potatoes but now they are in pasture. The fields were probably reseeded by spreading hay seeds or allowing the land to lie fallow. A large variety of native flowering plants is found in the fields including

Fig. 8.16
The Bog Commissioners, who were appointed to plan the reclamation of bogs, surveyed Mongan in 1810. Their map shows turf-cutting to the south. Lucky for Mongan that their proposals for drains (shown as dashed lines) were never implemented.

spotted orchids, meadow pea, yellow rattle, bulbous buttercup and cowslip, the last two indicating the effect of liming as they are usually found in dry limestone soils.

After the famine, reclamation slowed down and it has only recently gained momentum due to the availability of large machinery. Since the 1960s reclamation work has taken place on the north side near old bog gardens, but in contrast to the fields created in the last century these fields are of little natural history interest as they have been seeded with a standard grass clover mix.

UNRECLAIMED AREAS

Most of the marginal areas around the bog, which were cut for turf since the 19th century have not been reclaimed. These are called "cutaway" and can be found all

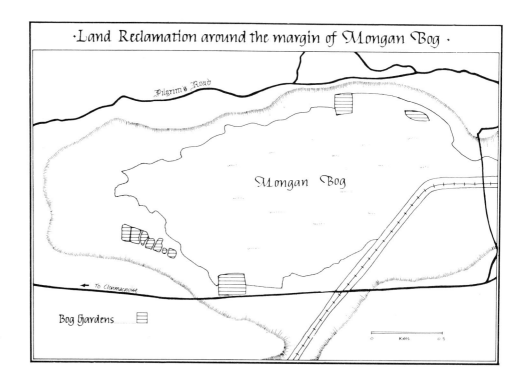

Fig. 8.17
The "bog gardens" around the margin of Mongan recall a period of farming history when, due to land shortage, farmers succeeded in turning uncut bog into productive fields.

around the edge of Mongan (fig. 8.18). The cutaway surface is very irregular, consisting of bare peat of varying wetness and some deep pools resulting from turf-cutting operations and vegetation in different stages of succession. Unfortunately the cutaway is also regarded as a local dumping ground.

The principal type of cutaway vegetation is a wet heath dominated by purple moor grass, a tussocky grass often seen in company with ling heather and cross-leaved heath. The oldest areas have been colonised by gorse, bog myrtle and trees. The latter include willows and birches but their growth is stunted by the lack of nutrients and frequent fires. Some of the pools have plants which are also seen on the bog, bladderwort and *Sphagnum* species; and others have exotic species like washing machines and fertilizer bags!

The insect fauna of the cutaway is much richer than that of the bog as there is a greater diversity of food plants but it does not appear to have any particular characteristics to distinguish it from that found in ditches anywhere in Clonmacnoise

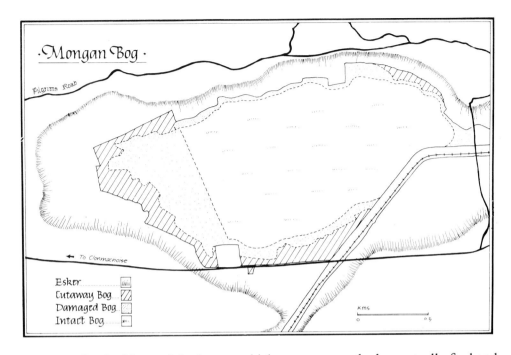

Fig. 8.18
"Cutaway" margins can be seen around all bogs. Their wildlife is very different from what is found on the intact bog surface.

or the Midlands. Many of the insects which are eaten on the bog actually feed and live in the cutaway.

THE FUTURE

As a result of centuries of interference by man in the form of reclamation, marginal drainage and fires as well as peat being removed, the bog surface has dried out in some areas and the typical plant community has disappeared.

The "facebanks" created by turf-cutters act as deep drains and so caused a narrow band at the margin to dry out but at the west end, where the bog is narrowest, the entire width has been affected. This process has also been hastened by the surface drains inserted by Bord Na Mona at either end of the bog. This work was carried out prior to the decision to conserve the site.

In areas affected by marginal drainage or surface drains, the pool hummock structure has disappeared and there are no open water pools. The vegetation is dominated by ling heather and cross-leaved heath (typical of the driest areas of the raised bog), there is little *Sphagnum* growth and few signs of the unique wildlife seen in the intact areas.

Drying worsens the effects of fires which are generally associated with turf-cutting or dumping. The bog is burnt to facilitate drying of the sods, to allow access to the peat or even to prevent another fire reaching the heaps of drying peat. Without any precautions being taken, the fires can spread rapidly. The western, drier end of the bog has been burnt four times since 1980. This has resulted in the almost complete disappearance of lichens and the presence of heather plants of uniform age, considerably younger than those found in the untouched bog.

The principal tasks facing conservationists are a) to prevent fires from reaching intact parts of the bog and b) limit the drying effects at the margin and the west end. If the intact areas deteriorate, plant and animal communities which have been present on the bog for the past thousands of years will eventually disappear.

Because of the studies being carried out by a large group of scientists at Mongan, it has became the best studied raised bog in the country. It has also attracted attention from film-makers. David Bellamy returned recently to film on the bog and commented favourably on its wetness!

Mongan is an internationally important site as irreplaceable as the National Monument. It needs to be managed as carefully to conserve its unique wildlife and as an example of a habitat which once covered a large proportion of the landscape of the midlands.

CHAPTER NINE

The Final Episode in the Story of (almost) all Bogs

Mary Tubridy

INTRODUCTION

To Irish people, bogs mean turf, either in the shape of the "auld sod" or in the sophisticated, sleek lines of the briquette. For people living beside them, the bog has always been a source of fuel and until the 1950s all turf in Clonmacnoise was cut by hand, using traditional methods and tools.

The scale of turf cutting changed in that decade when machinery became available to drain and cut entire bogs and Bord na Mona (The Turf Development Board) was set up to exploit Ireland's peat resources.

The company came to the Clonmacnoise area in 1953 and since then their operations have grown in several stages so that they produce a million tons of milled peat every year. Milled peat is a form of turf which is scraped from the surface of the bog.

Large scale exploitation of the bogs has generated much employment with Bord Na Mona and at the power station at Shannonbridge. As the midlands region has few sources of employment, this industry presently represents the only alternative to farming in the area (fig. 9.1). It has maintained the farming community as many landowners work full- or part-time and rely on these jobs to supplement a meagre farming income.

One can still see hand cutting, small scale mechanical cutting as well as the large-scale harvesting operation carried out by Bord na Mona in the Heritage Zone. For most bogs, this is the final chapter of their story.

Fig. 9.1
Bord Na Mona, based at Blackwater Works, owns 10,000 ha of peatland in the West Midlands. This land is serviced by 190 km of drains and a railway, 129 km long, transports the harvested peat to Shannonbridge Power Station.

THE WEATHER; ESSENTIAL INGREDIENT IN HARVESTING

Successful turf cutting relies completely on having dry windy weather to dry out the peat. When a sod is cut, it consists of 90% water but this must be halved if it is to be useful as fuel. As a result, harvesting is confined to a few months each year, and starts as early as April or May. The hand-cutter spends only a week on the bog early in the summer but large-scale cutting by Bord na Mona is carried on continuously until August or sometimes September. A visitor to Clonmacnoise will have a slim chance of seeing a hand-cutter working but depending on the weather he will probably see all the stages of large scale exploitation. As all the bogs in the area are being harvested in this way (with the exception of Mongan Bog), a vantage point on an esker ridge will provide a view of the operation.

TURF-CUTTING

In the last century the right to cut turf was given freely by landlords to tenants who farmed land bordering the bogs. This right, called "turbary" allowed turf-cutting on a particular length of the bog, indicated by shallow drains (called "lock spits") and once the peat was removed, the ground reverted to the use of the landlord.

The hand-cutter is now rare in Clonmacnoise but, when seen, he is probably using tools and cutting turf according to a method which has been handed down through several generations. His tools consist of a slean and spade; the latter is used to remove the top layer of vegetation ("scraw") from the top of the bank (fig. 9.2).

Fig. 9.2
Once a familiar site around Mongan: the sléan and barrow resting beside a rick of turf. Sléans can be bought in Shannonbridge for those who still have a taste for this work.

The peat is then cut horizontally along the "face bank", the exposed wall of peat, with the long-handled slean. This allows the cutting and removal of a sod with a single stroke. The sods are thrown on top of the bank and other members of the party, usually young children or women, spread them out to dry. If the weather is good, a few days cutting will usually supply enough turf for a household for a year.

After the sods have lain on the ground for a short time the family is sent back to the bog to place them in "stooks" (little piles of 4 - 5 sods). After a further series of visits during which they are placed in even larger piles, a large operation is launched; the turf is brought home and stored near the house.

MACHINE OR "SAUSAGE" TURF

Since 1980 a peculiar form of turf has been seen in Clonmacnoise. It usually looks like thick, brown strings lying on the bog in long parallel rows about 20 cm apart. It is "sausage" or "toothpaste turf" and it is cut using a tractor-mounted machine which has recently been developed by an Irish company.

The availability of the machine has meant that areas abandoned by hand turf-cutters in the sixties are now being cut by contractors who hire the machine to owners of the banks.

The "sausage" machine has numerous cutting blades which dig into the bog at an angle while it is being pulled by a tractor (fig. 9.3). The blades ensure that the upper, less valuable peat is mixed with the deeper (or fen) peat. This is then compressed and squeezed through extruders which leave a line of peat on the bog. A series of runs over the bog brings several rows to the surface. After a week or so, depending on the weather, the "sausages" are stooked and then dried in exactly the same way as sod peat.

BORD NA MONA OPERATIONS

The cut-over bogs present an awesome spectacle when viewed from the vantage point of an esker ridge. They are like vast brown deserts devoid of plants and animals. They come to life when fleets of huge machines, some 13m wide, emerge from their winter quarters to carry out the annual peat harvest.

Fig. 9.3
The blades of the "sausage machine" buried in the bog extract the peat through a narrow cut and this is then extruded, leaving behind the rows of peat which have given the sausage machine its name.

From the air, the brown dome of Mongan Bog can be distinguished from farmland and cut-over Blackwater Bog. The surface is dotted with hundreds of pools which increase each winter when the entire bog swells as it absorbs water.

Sphagnum or bog-moss is the most important plant on a raised bog. It thrives in the wet, acid conditions and its remains make up the bulk of the peat or turf.

One of the most attractive bog plants is bog rosemary. This is only found on raised bogs and for that reason has been named the County Offaly flower.

Pools on the bog are important habitats for aquatic plants and animals but as they are quite deep they should be treated with caution by bog explorers.

87

Fin Lough, lying beside cut-over Blackwater Bog, has become drier in the last 100 years and as a result reed beds have spread further into the lake.

OSCAR MERNE

DANIEL KELLY

The best time to visit a hazel woodland is in spring when the understorey plants such as bluebells (shown here), primroses, wood sorrel and orchids bloom and carpet the ground with colour.

MARY TUBRIDY

Lough Nanag, found along the western margin of Blackwater Bog half-way between Clonmacnoise and Shannonbridge, has almost disappeared due to the drainage work.

From its foundation, Bord na Mona operations have centred on the Midlands as raised bogs contain more substantial peat reserves than other types of bogs. The company is based in several "works" which were built near big bogs, all of which are linked to a power station. In Clonmacnoise, Bord na Mona operations are directed from the Blackwater Works (Uisce Dubh) which is 5 km east of the Shannonbridge power station to which it sells all the milled peat.

The workforce includes 574 full-time staff, and 198 seasonal workers who are employed for the annual harvest. The largest group of workers consists of drivers who operate the peat-harvesting machinery and among the total workforce of almost 800 are 4 female employees.

PREPARING THE BOG FOR LARGE-SCALE PEAT-HARVESTING

The first stage in exploitation on an intact bog involves extensive drainage works to release as much as half of the free water in the bog (fig. 9.4). The initial drainage work takes 5 — 6 years and after that time the water content of the peat will only have declined from 97% to 90%. The living growing surface layer of the bog has been killed as bog forming plants will not grow once a bog has been drained.

Fig. 9.4
The machinery used by BNM has been designed and built by the company. This drainage ditcher is in constant use during the harvesting season as drains must be deepened as the bog surface is lowered.

When ready for exploitation, the bog has been divided into production fields separated by drains 15 m apart which run the length of the bog. The centre field of each group of 11 fields is used to stockpile the harvested peat.

Fig. 9.5
Steps in peat harvesting.

Stage 1. The milled peat is first scraped from the surface using a machine called a miller which has three power driven spiked rollers.

Stage 2. A spoon harrow attached to a tractor passes up and down the field turning the peat.

THE HARVESTING PROCESS

The harvesting process involves a series of steps (fig. 9.5), many of which take place concurrently in each field. It is an impressive sight to see a fleet of similar, massive machines moving steadily in a line across the bog.

The process from scraping to stockpiling is called a harvest. In a good season 12 — 16 harvests may be taken from each bog, which will lower the bog by between 25 — 30cm. As the original depth of the peat is known at all the bogs, it has been possible to calculate their life expectancy. Blackwater Bog, which has been cut since the sixties, has a life expectancy of twenty years at current rates of development.

During the winter, the stockpiles are covered in polythene and remain on the bog until the peat is delivered to the power station by means of a narrow gauge railway which has been built by Bord na Mona. This links all the bogs with the power station and is carried over a new railway bridge built over the Shannon. Some of the track (roughly a quarter) is laid temporarily beside the stockpiles when the peat is being loaded on to the wagons for delivery to the power station (fig. 9.6).

FINAL DESTINATION — SHANNONBRIDGE POWER STATION

All the milled peat produced from the Blackwater group of bogs is delivered to Shannonbridge, which is the largest peat powered electricity generating station in Ireland (fig. 9.7). It became operational in 1965, twelve years after bog development work started and the Electricity Supply Board which owns the station now employs 176 people. Electricity output has expanded twice, in 1977 and 1982, with the addition of extra generating units. The boilers consume peat at the rate of 7,000 kg/hour and, when running at maximum capacity, the station can burn 1 million tons of peat each year.

As the station could not possibly store any sizeable reserves of peat, it is constantly being delivered by wagons. This is first fed into storage bunkers and then blended to ensure that it is suitably dry for the boilers. The boilers at the power station are similar to those used to burn low-grade coal with the additional first step that the peat must be dried and ground before being fed to the boilers.

There is an interesting postscript to the story of the final episode in the life of a peat bog. While most of the peat is burnt, a tiny amount escapes up the chimney. This fine ash settles in the surrounding area and has also been trapped in Mongan Bog forming a deposit which dates to the opening of the power station. Just as pollen grains preserved in the peat has provided an account of the vegetation history of the area, Mongan will also keep a record of the final destruction of all neighbouring bogs. Another event in the story of the landscape of Clonmacnoise has been recorded by the bog for future generations of bog scientists and historians to ponder about.

Stage 3. When the peat has dried sufficiently this machine forms a hill of dry peat in the centre of each field.

Stage 4. A harvesting machine with a 135 h.p. engine then moves the peat in a series of steps across the open drains to a stockpile in the centre of eleven fields.

A FUTURE FOR CUT-OVER PEATLANDS

When large scale peat cutting finishes in the Clonmacnoise area a huge amount of land will become available for other purposes (fig. 9.8). Its future use is uncertain as no agreed strategy exists for this resource. Research has been carried out to solve the technical problems associated with peatland forestry, agriculture and horticulture but future options will also need to take into account economic and social arguments. Another factor to be considered when examining the potential of any bog in the Shannon valley, is the problem of flooding once the base of the bog is reached, as it will be on or below the summer flood level. A system of dykes and pumps will be needed to prevent flooding and this will add a significant cost to any enterprise.

Fig. 9.6
Empty wagons on the railway line.

A mixture of activity is probably best for continued economic activity and employment. The following list indicates some possibilities:

1. **Agriculture.** It may be possible to extend carrying capacity if peat-cutting is locally curtailed.

2. **Horticulture.** This enterprise could be developed if local markets expand. Protected horticulture might be a better option if a source of thermal energy became available e.g. heat pumps from peat ponds or from "low temperature" thermal springs.

3. **Forestry.** It may be worth exploring industrial uses of willow, poplar and alder for baskets and crates and other products such as charcoal. Large-scale "industrial" hearvesting of reeds, may be feasible if products and markets are found, e.g. matting, packing, containers, as well as "traditional" thatching materials.

4. **Fish-Farming.** Marine fish culture and cell culture are going through a testing period of development. Fresh water fisheries, yielding coarse fish mainly, can be sustained where markets exist.

5. **Game.** Wetland game species, especially wild duck, can command good prices, if the market is developed.

6. **Tourism.** The visitors to the Norfolk Broads essentially visit flooded cutover peatlands. The midlands have already a diversity of rivers, lakes and canals but water-based activity of other kinds could be developed in large shallow lakes. In this case, landscape planning would ideally accompany the last stages of exploitation of the peat.

Fig. 9.7 Shannonbridge Power Station. Its hot water discharges indirectly increase the number and size of fish near the outfall, much to the satisfaction of anglers.

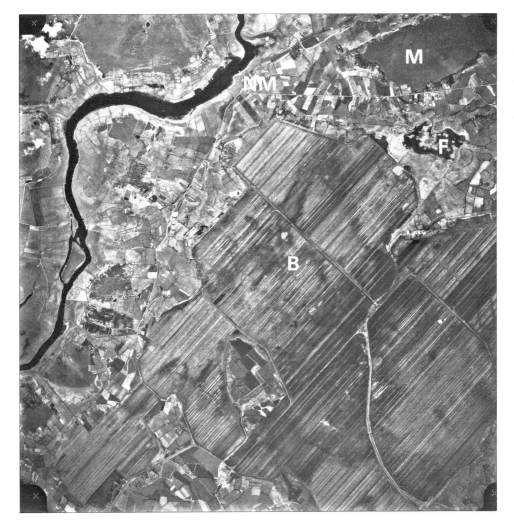

Fig. 9.8
An aerial photograph reveals the extent of cutover bogs now being worked by Bord Na Mona (M = Mongan Bog; B = Blackwater Bog; F = Fin Lough; N.M. = National Monument.)

7. **Nature Conservation.** This activity is an integral part of education, cultural development, amenity and tourism. In designing a cutover landscape, opportunities should be sought for protection of existing features of interest and cration of new ones. The flooding of the acid peatland with calcareous riverwater would create many ecological habitats.

CHAPTER TEN

The Natural History of Eskers

Daniel Kelly and David Jeffrey

INTRODUCTION

To farmers in the Heritage Zone, eskers are the most useful areas on their land, and the history of farming is largely the story of land use on eskers. Their usefulness is not confined to farming: they supply sand and gravel for building and roadmaking and from earliest times eskers have provided sites for houses, roads and settlements. Esker wildlife is also of significance, in particular woodlands and species-rich grasslands. Understanding all the resources eskers can provide will contribute to their wise use, the best definition of conservation.

THE HISTORY OF ESKER VEGETATION

The history of vegetation in Clonmacnoise (Chapter 2) indicates that prior to 3,000 B.C. all the dry land in the Heritage Zone was covered with forest. In the esker woodlands and in areas such as the Rocks of Clorhane, the principal trees were oak, hazel and elm. These woodlands were gradually whittled away, as more and more land was cleared for tillage and pasture. By roughly 300 A.D. the greater part of the eskers had been cleared of forest.

However, through Early Christian and Medieval times timber remained extremely important in the local economy suggesting that substantial woodlands remained in some areas. The early buildings at Clonmacnoise were constructed of timber; apparently stone became popular as a building material only when suitable timber was no longer available. The Down Survey Map of about 1650 A.D. (fig. 10.1) is our first limited record of land use in the Heritage Zone, which shows that there

were still woods on the eskers as well as woody pastures and shrubby areas ("shr").
Woody pastures were open woods where cattle and other livestock were allowed to
graze. Other woods were probably fenced against livestock, to protect saplings and
coppice regrowth from browsing animals.

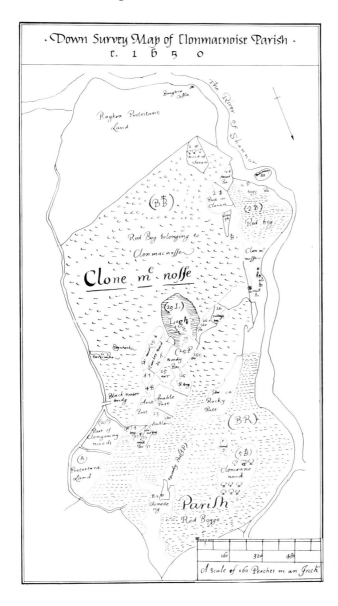

Fig. 10.1
After Cromwell's victory
maps covering the whole
country were required to
catalogue the lands which
he had confiscated from his
Catholic opponents. These
maps, later called the Down
Survey maps, were drawn
up by surveyors recruited
from among the disbanded
military and Trinity College
students.

ESKER GRASSLANDS

The commonest vegetation on the eskers today is grassland and the most important type is a species-rich grassland similar to that found in many parts of Europe, including the chalk grasslands of southern England and the valleys in Alpine regions. Collectively these are called oat grass-fescue swards, of which there are many variants. They are largely confined to light, dry soils derived from lime-rich rocks.

Grasslands they may be, but the array of broad-leaved flowering plants surpasses the range of grass species. In the Heritage Zone, almost 100 different plants have been recorded on eskers of which only eighteen are grasses. As a result of the large number of broad-leaved flowering plants the range of colour in an esker pasture or meadow is always an impressive sight. There is the spectacle of white and gold dog-daisies, purple devil's bit scabious, the pink of meadow clover and valerian, the yellow of bird's foot trefoil and even the green flowers of lady's mantle (fig. 10.2). A similar scene is frequently captured on postcards from the Alps.

In primeval times these light-demanding species would have been found in forest clearings, which arose through natural events such as storms or fires started by lightning strikes. In Ireland grazing animals such as red deer and hares would have browsed among the clearings and slowed down the regrowth of trees. When man finally cleared the trees, he expanded the area of suitable habitat for these species.

ESKER SOILS

The fundamental characteristics of esker soil influence the composition of the plant community whether woodland, grassland or scrub. The esker soil is composed mainly of calcareous sand, gravel and stones with some finer and less calcareous material. This gives rise to soils which may collectively be described as rendzina type (rendzina is a Polish work reflecting the sound the plough makes when it hits bedrock or stones). They are most obvious on the ridge of the esker and are shallow soils with a darker topmost layer, rich in organic matter. On the sides of the eskers, the steep slopes encourage slippage of the gravelly material so that the soils are maintained in an immature state. As a result of the slope, the soils sometimes drain so freely that they are subject to drought.

Bird's foot trefoil

Great Knapweed

Dog Daisy

Fig. 10.2
Common plants of esker pastures.

There is some variation within this general soil type, in particular to a soil associated with the Clonfinlough esker. Acidic patches are found here and elsewhere which carry the acid loving species wavy hairgrass (*Deschampsia flexuosa*) and ling heather.

PRODUCTIVITY OF ESKER GRASSLANDS

While the esker grasslands are not highly productive, they are good sources of cut and grazed forage. This forage provides the correct balance between protein, digestible dry matter and minerals but only if it is managed carefully by farmers. Most of the mineral content is supplied not by the grasses but by the broad-leaved herbs whose growth can be depressed by incorrect timing and rates of fertilizer application. Herbs such as yarrow or ribwort plantain have more than four times the magnesium, three times the calcium, up to twice the potassium and one and a half times the phosphorus of the common esker grasses. Legumes such as the various clovers, lady's fingers vetch (*Anthyllis*) and bird's foot trefoil are rich in protein as they can fix nitrogen, but this ability to fix nitrogen can be depressed by excess use of nitrogen fertilizer.

Another subtle feature of esker grasslands which affects farming practice is that fertilizer minerals behave differently. Nitrogen, unless applied at the time of early growth, is rapidly lost into the groundwater because the soil is very free-draining. Similarly, potassium is easily lost because of a general absence of clay minerals in the soil. Phosphorus, on the other hand, is bound firmly to the calcium carbonate of the gravel but is made available slowly through the agency of mycorrhizal fungi associated with the roots of almost all grassland plants.

PASTURES AND MEADOWS

Pastures are permanent grasslands, usually grazed by drystock. The grazing animal is an active agent for the re-cycling of all minerals which return to the soil as urine and dung (fig. 10.3). The minerals removed as liveweight gain are usually less than 10% of the total yearly turnover from plants to animals to soil. This recycling of urine and dung may give rise to large and small-scale patchiness in the vegetation of the pasture. Areas which receive disproportionate amounts of dung may eventually develop into nettle beds and elder thickets, as it is known that these plants require high quantities of phosphate and nitrogen.

Fig. 10.3
The nitrogen cycle in a
permanent pasture.

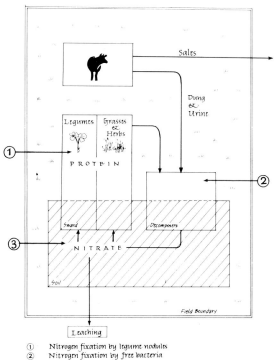

PASTURE

① Nitrogen fixation by legume nodules
② Nitrogen fixation by free bacteria
③ Fertilizer and fixed nitrogen in rainfall

The continuous cropping of plants by the cutting teeth of cattle eliminates tall plants. It also encourages the grasses as there is a zone of growth at the base of each leaf, and cropping tends to stimulate growth of the remainder of the leaf and of additional shoots called tillers (a broad-leaved herb, when grazed, can resprout only from the buds, if any, in the angle between leaf and stem). Grazing is also selective so that plants with physical defences such as thistles and brambles, and plants with chemical defences (i.e. poisonous plants) such as ragwort and buttercups, are avoided by stock and will be at an advantage in a grazed pasture. Legumes are sought by stock along with the more succulent grasses such as cocksfoot.

In a meadow (i.e. a field which is cut for hay or silage), the mineral cycle is rather different, even though the area may be grazed for brief periods after mowing (fig. 10.4). Farming practices in traditional hay-meadows, mown as weather permits in

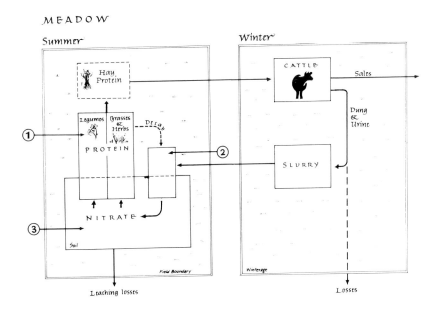

Fig. 10.4
The nitrogen cycle in a
meadow.

June or July, encourage tall herbs and early- flowering species. During the spring-to-summer period of growth, many biological activities take place, which renew the fertility of the soil. Plant remains are broken down by fungi, bacteria and soil animals, which leads to mineral release. Nitrogen is fixed by soil bacteria, by bacteria on root surfaces and by the specialised legume system. Even if the meadows are not grazed by man's domesticated animals, grazing of other kinds is evident, e.g. by leaf-chewing beetles and hares, by sap sucking greenfly and leaf bugs. As the forage is cut, plant material and minerals are bodily removed from the meadows, breaking the "natural" cycle completely. If cattle dung is later spread on the land some of these minerals will be returned to keep and maintain the cycle.

SUCCESSION: FROM GRASSLAND TO WOODLAND

The grassland on the eskers arose through woodland clearance; its continued existence depends on a regime of mowing and grazing. Where management diminishes, pastures tend to be invaded by taller-growing plants that are avoided by grazing animals: chiefly spiny shrubs such as gorse, blackthorn, bramble, hawthorn and wild rose (fig. 10.5). Blackthorn invades fields from the margins, advancing out from the hedges by

Fig. 10.5 Woodland succession

a
The present vegetation on on the eskers is predominantly grassland which is maintained by grazing and mowing.

b
Without management, grassland will be invaded by spiny plants such as gorse which are not eaten by stock. Farmers often try to remove gorse by burning but the plants quickly regrow from the base.

c
Tree seedlings (such as those of hazel) have a chance of surviving within an open spiny scrub. The spines deter grazing animals, yet the young plants receive sufficient light.

d
The final stage in succession is a mixed woodland of oak, ash and hazel, all of which probably started life as seedlings within a spiny scrub. Seedlings of large trees have less chance of surviving in a hazel wood, hence the transition from hazel woodland to oak/ash woodland takes a long time.

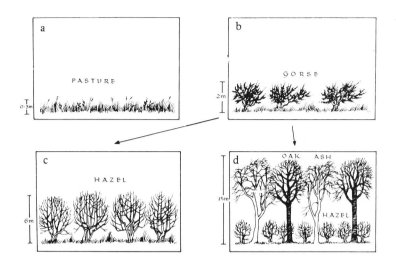

suckering, and soon — if not cut back — forming an impenetrable thicket. Gorse (or furze or whin, *Ulex europaeus*) seeds into open land, especially on steeper slopes and poorer soils, forming extensive bushy patches. These provide a blaze of golden, sweet-scented blossom in April and May.

Seedlings of trees and non-spiny shrubs have no chance of survival in a normal pasture: they are far too palatable to livestock. If, however, such seedlings spring up among already-established spiny plants, they have a chance: the spines of their neighbours may protect them. The first species to come in by this stratagem is usually hazel, which grows into a large shrub or small tree, commonly 5-7 m high (fig. 10.5c). At several locations in the Heritage Zone we can find old, scraggy-looking bushes of gorse, overtopped by hazel; clearly the hazel has outgrown and suppressed the very plants whose spines once helped it to survive. This process by which, through the course of time, one species ousts and replaces another is called succession. The low spiny shrubs such as gorse are "pioneers" in the succession; the end-point of the succession, the "climax", is a woodland dominated by deciduous trees such as oak and ash (fig. 10.5d). Like hazel, these trees seem to have the best chance of establishment among low spiny shrubs.

Most woods in the Heritage Zone today are very small, scattered along the eskers. It seems clear that all are secondary woodland, i.e. they have developed on land that

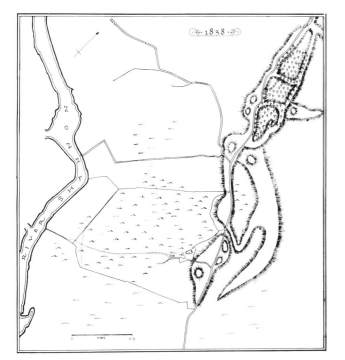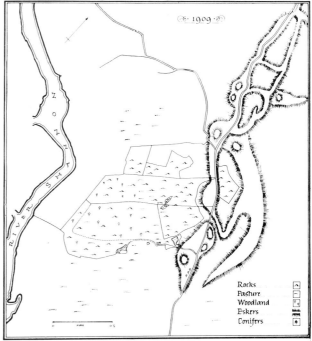

was once cleared of forest and converted to agricultural use; subsequent neglect has allowed shrubs and trees to recolonise. Study of successive Ordnance Survey maps shows a "kaleidoscope" of scattered patches of scrub and woodland, disappearing at one place and springing up at another. Of the five principal areas of woodland of the present day, none has remained undisturbed over the past century. In the woodland near "The Rocks of Clorhane" (fig. 10.6), the southern half became wooded between 1838 and 1884, and now supports woodland of hazel, ash and pedunculate oak. The northern half was still largely pasture in 1909-10; it is now a thicket of blackthorn, i.e. it is still at an early stage in the succession.

Fig. 10.6
Woodland on the "Rocks of Clorhane" and adjacent esker in 1838 and 1909.

THE ESKER WOODS

The five main stands in the Heritage Zone today are privately owned, but all but one can be viewed from the public road. All stands are dominated by hazel. Ash and pedunculate oak are the commonest of the larger trees; downy birch and hawthorn

Fig. 10.7
Early purple orchids are conspicuous in woodland and hedges in April and May.

Fig. 10.8
The flowering spike of Lords and Ladies is adapted to lure and trap midges in order to bring about cross-pollination. Only a few manage to escape its depths.

(usually known in Ireland as 'whitethorn' or 'may') are also common. The trees are modest in stature, the tallest being generally no more than 13-15 m high. The best developed wood (in 1984) contained 14 species of trees and large shrubs: to the five already mentioned, we add holly, spindle-tree, common sally, goat willow, blackthorn, elder (known locally as tromán, a diminutive of trom, the standard name in Irish), and, at the margins, wych elm, wild damson and dwarf cherry. The last two are introduced species; wild damson was formerly grown for its plum-like fruits but is now no longer cultivated.

The ground flora of these woods is rich in herbaceous plants. Most of these flower in April and May, before the trees expand their canopy of leaves and intercept much of the light before it can reach the woodland floor. Primroses and violets, wood-sorrel and wood-anemone, wild strawberries, early purple orchids (fig. 10.7) and bluebells, form a kaleidoscope of delicate hues that has, however, completely vanished by mid-summer. Lords-and-ladies (also called cuckoo-pint and other curious names) produces in April its weird green and purple flower-spikes (fig. 10.8). By late summer all the green parts of the plant have died down, leaving bare spikes of scarlet berries; like all parts of the plant, these are poisonous to humans. They are eaten by blackbirds and thrushes; the seeds pass through the gut unharmed and the birds thus act as dispersal agents for the plant.

In an agricultural landscape, even small woods provide refuge for many kinds of wildlife, from the smallest to the largest. Of all the habitats in the Heritage Zone, woodland is the richest habitat for bird species, because of the diversity of available food, shelter and nest sites. Some birds, such as the shy woodcock, are more or less confined to the woods; others find a similar habitat in hedges.

Much of the esker woods and their margins are heavily grazed and trampled by cattle; this makes it very difficult for tree saplings to survive, and could jeopardize the long-term future of the woods.

CLORHANE WOOD

The wood at Clorhane differs from others in the Heritage Zone in its size, and in the nature of the terrain (fig. 10.9). It is underlain by a remarkable stretch of

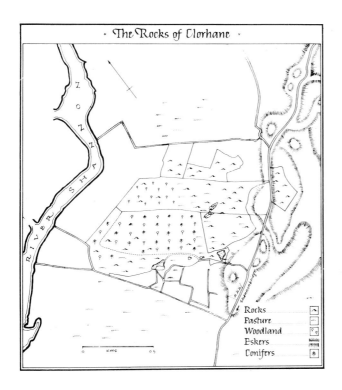

· The Rocks of Clorhane ·

Rocks
Pasture
Woodland
Eskers
Conifers

Fig. 10.9
Present-day woodland on
the "Rocks of Clorhane."

(a) The Yew Tree

(b) Branch from
male tree

(c) Branch from female tree,
showing developing seed, and pink
cup-shaped aril surrounding
mature seed

Fig. 10.10
Yew is a particularly slow-
growing tree which is rarely
found near pastures as
nearly all parts of the plant
are poisonous to livestock.

outcropping limestone rock — a Burren in miniature. The "Wood of Cloran" is clearly marked on the Down Survey Map of 1654 (fig. 10.1). However, by the early 19th century the area had apparently been completely cleared, leaving only rough grassland and bare rock. In the course of the present century native shrubs and trees have gradually recolonised a large part of the area. In the 1960's much of the southern part was planted up with introduced species — conifers and beech.

Today the native woodland occupies some 22 hectares; it is mostly well-developed hazel scrub, 5-9 m high, with an admixture of other trees and shrubs. Yew is frequent over a small area of semi-open "pavement" (fig. 10.10). This colony is of considerable interest as yew is, or was, a species characteristic of rocky limestone areas. Yew was abundant in the Burren itself in prehistoric times but is now rare there. The only substantial yew wood in Ireland today is in the Killarney National Park in Co. Kerry.

Unlike the esker woods, the Clorhane woodland is largely ungrazed and the ground flora is well-developed. Perhaps the most remarkable feature of this woodland is the extraordinarily luxuriant growth of mosses. The lower parts of the trees and the rock outcrops are swathed in a thick mossy growth, such as one would expect to find only in the wettest regions of the west and south-west of Ireland. This would suggest that Clorhane has an unusual local 'microclimate' with exceptionally high humidity levels; further investigation is called for.

On the zoological side, the site is exceptionally rich in moth species, some of which had not hitherto been recorded in Ireland outside the Burren region. Local sources suggest that pine martens may have been present in the recent past, although they have not been sighted in the past five years.

Fig. 10.11
While only a few small woodlands can now be found in the Heritage Zone, these are used by farmers to provide shelter for animals and as a source of timber. Their conservation would allow for their continued use by their owners.

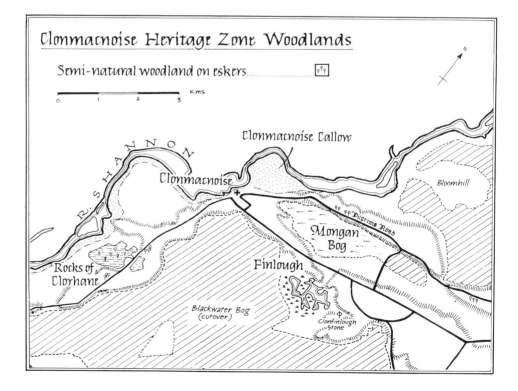

WOODLAND CONSERVATION AND MANAGEMENT

The little woods in the Heritage Zone today are only a faint reflection of the great forests that once covered the area (fig. 10.11). However, even as they are, their educational and scientific value is considerable. They provide a refuge for the native woodland flora and fauna in a landscape where woodland is very scarce. The Heritage Zone woods provide an interesting diversity in substratum (esker, limestone outcrop), in age, and in management regime (from overgrazed to virtually ungrazed).

Many other small woods shown on the Ordnance Survey maps have since been obliterated. As a recent instance, a formerly substantial area of woodland on the esker slope between Mongan Bog and the Pilgrim's Road was completely destroyed in the year 1980. The future of the surviving woods is far from secure. Yet it is vital to safeguard them if we wish to maintain the diversity of natural habitats that is such an exciting feature of the Heritage Zone today. If the present day woodlands are conserved and grazing and felling controlled, canopies of full-grown trees would in time develop. These reflections of the former forests would survive to enlighten future generations.

○
David Jeffrey is the director of the Heritage Zone Study and is a senior lecturer in biology in Trinity College.
○
Daniel Kelly is a member of the Heritage Zone Study Group and a lecturer in the Botany Department of Trinity College.

CHAPTER ELEVEN

Changing Lifestyles on the Farm

Mary Tubridy

Fig. 11.1
Some of the cottage style houses still inhabited in the Clonmacnoise area.

FARMING IN 1830

One can get a picture of the number of farms in Clonmacnoise in the last century by locating single storey cottages which dot the area. Most of these are now in ruins, some have become outhouses and only a few survive as farmhouses (fig. 11.1). These were the houses lived in by the people of Clonmacnoise 150 years ago when the population was roughly three to four times its present level. They were built of rough cut stone and mortar, roofed with thatch and all had an open fire which was kept lighting continuously and sent its smoke through a hole in a roof. Each farm supported about six people, probably spanning a few generations, who all lived in this three roomed cottage.

While most households had farms attached, there was a large number of landless people. Some were craftsmen, shoemakers, harnessmen, carpenters and smiths and their assistants, but most were farm labourers who worked long hours (6a.m. — 6p.m. in summer) for poor wages and who managed to survive only if their employer also provided them with a small patch on which to grow potatoes. This group created the "bog gardens" described in Chapter 8 and were almost wiped out by the famine.

All the land in Clonmacnoise belonged to several landlords (all living outside the area) who included the Church of Ireland Bishop of Meath who had acquired monastery land 250 years earlier. Two farmers living in the area did not pay rent, the Church of Ireland rector who lived at the glebe house in Carrowkeel, Clonfinlough, and a Mr. Coghlan who also farmed 200 acres at Clonfinlough. The rector was

VALUATION OF TENEMENTS.
PARISH OF CLONMACNOISE.

140

No. and Letters of Reference to Map.	Townlands and Occupiers.	Immediate Lessors.	Description of Tenement.	Area. A. R. P.	Land. £ s. d.	Buildings. £ s. d.	Total Annual Valuation of Rateable Property. £ s. d.
	CLONLYON GLEBE—*continued.*						
16	Martin Milleny, .	Rev. James Alexander,	Land, . .	7 0 37	2 15 0	—	2 15 0
	Martin Milleny,		House, offices, & land,	56 2 18	10 15 0	1 5 0	12 0 0
17 {a,b,c}	Patrick Loonan,	Same, .	House, offices, & land,		7 15 0	0 15 0	8 10 0
	Michael Milleny,		House, offices, & land,		5 15 0	1 5 0	7 0 0
18	James Hynes, .	Same, .	House and land,	8 1 20	4 0 0	0 10 0	4 10 0
19 A	Michael Molloy, .	Same, .	Land, .	13 1 31	11 0 0	—	12 15 0
— B				3 3 7	1 15 0	—	
— A d	Vacant, .	Michael Molloy,	House and office.	—	—	0 15 0	0 15 0
	Denis Gorman, .	Rev. Jas. Alexander,	House, office, and land,	13 1 21	7 0 0	1 0 0	9 10 0
20 A			Land, .	3 2 2	1 10 0	—	
— B	Patrick Molloy,		Land, .	8 1 25	2 5 0	—	2 5 0
21 A	Michael Molloy,		Land, .		2 5 0	—	2 5 0
	Patrick Molloy,		House, office, & land,	9 0 22	2 10 0	1 0 0	3 10 0
— B {a,b}	Michael Molloy,	Same, .	House, offices, & land,		2 10 0	1 10 0	4 0 0
	Patrick Molloy,		Land, .	4 3 34	1 0 0	—	1 0 0
— C	Michael Molloy,		Land, .		1 0 0	—	1 0 0
	Patrick Molloy,		Land, .	8 3 25	1 10 0	—	1 10 0
— D	Michael Molloy,		Land, .		1 10 0	—	1 10 0
	Michael Molloy,		Land, .		4 15 0	—	4 15 0
22 {a,b,c}	Patrick Caulfield,	Same, .	House, office, & land,	52 2 32	7 0 0	1 0 0	8 0 0
	John Caulfield,		House, office, & land,		7 0 0	1 0 0	8 0 0
	Sarah Caulfield,		House, office, & land,		4 15 0	0 10 0	5 5 0
23 {a,b,c}	Patrick Devery,	Same, .	House and land,	28 3 34	4 5 0	1 0 0	5 5 0
	Keiran Devery,		House and land,		4 5 0	1 0 0	5 5 0
	Timothy Devery,		House and land,		5 0 0	1 5 0	6 5 0
24 {a,b}	James Dolan,	Same, .	House, office, & land,	23 0 38	5 0 0	1 5 0	6 5 0
	John Dolan,		House, office, & land,				
			Total, .	886 3 24	242 4 0	36 14 0	278 18 0
	CLONMACNOISE— (*Ord. S. 5 & 6.*)						
	Michael Curly,				4 5 0	—	4 5 0
	Thomas Connor, .				2 0 0	—	2 0 0
	Michael Kilmartin,				1 0 0	—	1 0 0
	Edward Darcy,				3 5 0	—	3 5 0
	Patrick Darcy, .				1 10 0	—	1 10 0
	Thomas Darcy, . .				1 0 0	—	1 0 0
	Peter Darcy, .				1 0 0	—	1 0 0
	Anne Merrigan, . .				1 0 0	—	1 0 0
	Michl. Flannery, sen.,				1 0 0	—	1 0 0
	Michl. Flannery, jun.,				1 0 0	—	1 0 0
	Hugh O'Neill, .				1 5 0	—	1 5 0
	Bryan Donohoe, .				1 5 0	—	1 5 0
	Capt. Wm. Johnston,				11 15 0	—	11 15 0
	Terence Daly, .				2 15 0	—	2 15 0
	Francis Egan, .				0 10 0	—	0 10 0
1	John Daly, .	Arthur M'Guinness, .	Land, ...	76 2 0	1 10 0	—	1 10 0
	Bridget M'Manus,				0 10 0	—	0 10 0
	Thomas M'Manus, .				0 10 0	—	0 10 0
	Patrick Horan, .				0 15 0	—	0 15 0
	Terence M'Manus,				1 5 0	—	1 5 0
	James M'Manus, .				0 15 0	—	0 15 0
	Stephen Flannery,				1 0 0	—	1 0 0
	Patrick Flannery,				1 5 0	—	1 5 0
	Patrick Daly, .				1 10 0	—	1 10 0
	Patrick Molloy, .				3 5 0	—	3 5 0
	John Kelly, .				0 10 0	—	0 10 0
	Michl. Devery, sen.,				1 0 0	—	1 0 0
	Michl. Devery, jun.,				1 0 0	—	1 0 0
	Keran Devery, .				1 0 0	—	1 0 0
	Edward Kilmartin,				1 0 0	—	1 0 0
	James Kilmartin,				1 0 0	—	1 0 0
2 d	Captn. Wm. Johnston,	Lord Bishop of Meath and —— M'Gusty,	House, offices, and land,	364 2 16	164 0 0	15 0 0	179 0 0
— b	Michael Brennan, .	Captn. Wm. Johnston,	House and garden, .	0 1 0	0 4 0	1 1 0	1 5 0
3	Michael Hubbart, .	Same, . .	House and land, .	7 0 23	2 10 0	1 0 0	3 10 0
4	Loughlin Egan, .	Same, . .	House and land, .	1 0 24	0 15 0	0 10 0	1 5 0

Fig. 11.2
Griffith's valuation compiled in the mid-nineteenth century, provides a list of all the occupants of land and buildings, the area of the holding and a description of the building. This section covers the National Monument and the Clonmacnoise callow.

supported principally by the tithes paid by the farming community which were based on acreages of wheat, oats, barley and flax sown and numbers of sheep. All the remaining land was divided into small holdings of 2 — 15 acres which were let on a yearly basis for between 1/2 and 2 guineas (fig. 11.2).

While there are no records for the period, which are comparable with the statistics available for the twentieth century, accounts written by observers and visitors provide a picture of farming in the area which compares with other parts of Ireland in the early 19th century. Mixed farming was common and tillage, particularly potato-growing was far more important than at any other time. As spuds and milk were eaten once or twice a day, a proportionately large area of the farm was used for potatoes and this land was always the most fertile available. As well as oats for horse-feed, wheat and barley were grown to pay the rent and flax was sown for linen.

Cows provided the other ingredients of the staple diet and some farmers had one rarely two. Like the cows, the other farm animals (the most important of which were pigs and sheep), belonged to the "old breeds" and had not been crossed with foreign types. Fish from Fin Lough or the Shannon added some variety to the diet and fat bacon was considered a treat at Christmas. Land was fertilised and limed by dunging and marling, but the practice of "boiting", (paring and burning the soil and vegetation) was still common, much to the disapproval of the landlords.

A large farmer may have owned a horse-drawn plough and harrow (fig. 11.3) but on most of the farms each season's work was done by hand. The spade was used to make drills for potatoes or corn, the scythe or sickle for hay making and reaping, the rake for turning and the flail for thrashing. Many of the "lazy beds" made by the spade are still recognisable on the eskers as shallow parallel ridges. Schools were deserted in Spring and Autumn when everyone was required to work on the farm.

Fig. 11.3
This harrow was hailed as an innovation around the 1800s.

From his shoes and socks to his jacket, the farmer's clothes were probably manufactured in Clonmacnoise. Wool from sheep was woven by a local weaver into grey frieze, a type of coarse woollen cloth which was used to make jackets, trousers and shirts. The wool was also knitted into socks. All of this work, spinning, weaving and knitting, was done by women and girls who sold the excess to neighbours or at the weekly market in Shannonbridge. The community was almost self-sufficient except for exotic

Fig. 11.4
A Lawrence collection
photograph of the scholars
who attended the hedge
school which was located in
the cellar of the Cathedral,
the largest ruined church in
Clonmacnoise.

items like tobacco or snuff. The landless class moved frequently from place to place but few members of families left the area, except perhaps in the case of marriage.

Schooling took place entirely within the parish. There were three "hedge schools" which had 120 — 200 pupils depending on the season and the demands of the farm (fig. 11.4). The income of the teachers depended not only on the weather, but on the proficiency of the pupils, as they charged 1/8d (= 8p). quarterly to teach reading and spelling but 3/4d (= 17p) for writing and arithmetic. There was a small Protestant school which was attended by the children of the few Protestant families who lived in the parish. Everyone understood English but Irish was still spoken, particularly within earshot of the landlord's agent or tithe collector!

Any surplus from the farm was sold at markets and fairs, mainly at Shannonbridge which was then a large town , containing 280 houses, but Clonmacnoise also had its own fair on September 17th to coincide with Pattern Day. At the fair in Shannonbridge the farmer may have sold a pig or calf and other livestock, wool, corn or pottles of flax. After striking a deal, he may have visited one of the "shebeens" in the village or eaten at the only inn.

1930; ONE HUNDRED YEARS LATER

The population of Clonmacnoise still relied completely on farming in 1930 but there were fewer people than in 1830 and farms were larger. The average farm now consisted of 17 acres. Some of the land on the farm had been farmed by previous generations of the family but the difference between 1930 and 1830 was that the manager was now the owner of the land. Through State intervention, tenants had been helped to acquire their holdings from the landlords and as a result, landlords and their agents had disappeared from Clonmacnoise. Tithes were no longer paid and the income earned was used solely to pay off the low interest loan taken out to buy the holding. Farms were larger as the famine and its aftermath had caused a decline in the population and many holdings had been amalgamated.

A specialised type of farming had emerged by 1930 which centred around dry stock. Calves were bought in when a few weeks or months old (generally from the west of Ireland) and then kept until they were two or three. Almost 90% of the land was laid out in permanent pasture to feed these cattle and a few milch cows. As flax was no longer grown, people now bought some materials for clothes but each household was still self-sufficient in meat, milk, vegetables and fuel (fig. 11.5). The horse was used for farmwork and each farm had one or two horses and perhaps a pony and trap to bring the family to Mass or the shops. Dunlop had invented the pneumatic tyre and many of these bounced around the roads of Clonmacnoise as bicycles were the commonest means of transport.

Oats were grown for horses and each family cultivated a patch of potatoes which were cooked in a 3-legged pot (fig. 11.6). Vegetables also included turnips and cabbage for the household and mangels, kale and field cabbage for animals. One farmer was growing an acre of rye either as animal feed or to supply straw for thatching. Sheep were very common and every household had a pig which enjoyed much care and attention as it supplied meat for the family. Housed only at night it was fattened

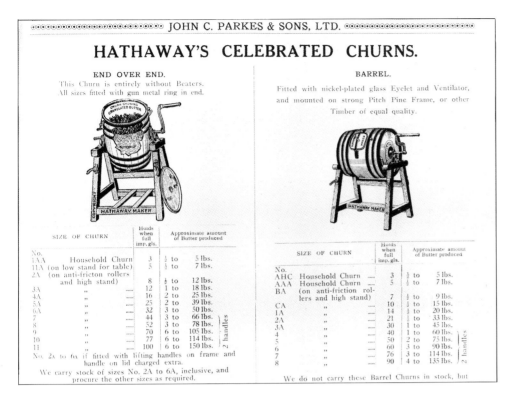

⊙⊙⊙⊙⊙⊙⊙⊙⊙⊙⊙⊙⊙⊙⊙⊙⊙⊙⊙⊙⊙ JOHN C. PARKES & SONS, LTD. ⊙⊙⊙⊙⊙⊙⊙⊙⊙⊙⊙⊙⊙⊙⊙⊙⊙⊙⊙⊙⊙⊙

HATHAWAY'S CELEBRATED CHURNS.

END OVER END.
This Churn is entirely without Beaters.
All sizes fitted with gun metal ring in end.

BARREL.
Fitted with nickel-plated glass Eyelet and Ventilator,
and mounted on strong Pitch Pine Frame, or other
Timber of equal quality.

SIZE OF CHURN		Holds when full imp. gls.	Approximate amount of Butter produced
No.			
1AA	Household Churn	3	½ to 5 lbs.
1A (on low stand for table)		5	½ to 7 lbs.
2A (on anti-friction rollers and high stand)		8	½ to 12 lbs.
3A	"	12	1 to 18 lbs.
4A	"	16	2 to 25 lbs.
5A	"	25	2 to 39 lbs.
6A	"	32	3 to 50 lbs.
7	"	44	3 to 66 lbs.
8	"	52	3 to 78 lbs.
9	"	70	6 to 105 lbs.
10	"	77	6 to 114 lbs.
11	"	100	6 to 150 lbs.

No. 2A to 6A if fitted with lifting handles on frame and
handle on lid charged extra.
We carry stock of sizes No. 2A to 6A, inclusive, and
procure the other sizes as required.

SIZE OF CHURN		Holds when full imp. gls.	Approximate amount of Butter produced
No.			
AHC	Household Churn	3	½ to 5 lbs.
AAA	Household Churn	5	½ to 7 lbs.
BA	(on anti-friction rollers and high stand)	7	½ to 9 lbs.
CA	"	10	½ to 15 lbs.
1A	"	14	½ to 20 lbs.
2A	"	21	½ to 33 lbs.
3A	"	30	1 to 45 lbs.
4	"	40	1 to 60 lbs.
5	"	50	2 to 75 lbs.
6	"	60	3 to 90 lbs.
7	"	76	3 to 114 lbs.
8	"	90	4 to 135 lbs.

We do not carry these Barrel Churns in stock, but

Fig. 11.5
A page from Parkes,
catalogue showing the style
of churn on offer to the
dairyman in 1930. Parkes
were the biggest importers
of farm equipment at that
time.

on skimmed milk, yellow meal and titbits it foraged outdoors as it had the freedom
of the fields except when farrowing. Killing the pig, which was an earshattering ordeal,
was an annual event of spine tingling significance from which many neighbours
benefitted and most of the pig's flesh finally became smoked bacon after months of
hanging in the chimney breast above the turf fire. The traditional-style farmhouse
now had glass in the windows and nearby roamed gaggles of geese, dragoons of ducks
and endless numbers of hens. They provided Sunday dinners and surplus stock was
sold to shops in Athlone and Shannonbridge.

1980; RECENT FARMING PRACTICES

Almost everyone in Clonmacnoise still lives on a farm but few households derive
all their income from farming. Almost invariably a man from the household also works
for Bord na Mona or the Electricity Supply Board and this job provides most of

3-legged Pot

Pot Oven

Griddle

Fig. 11.6
Pans for boiling and cooking
over an open fire.

111

the family income. Financial security means that a new house can be built and the farm can be modernised. Without this source of employment the area would be far more sparsely populated and the general level of income would be considerably lower. Employment in these industries has succeeded in arresting the population decline which had occurred since 1840: from 1960 to the 1980's the population of the area has been steady at almost 300 people.

The farms are still small even though there have been several redistributions of land since 1930. The average size of farm is double the area it was in 1930, almost 35 acres. Each farm is still owned and managed by the same family and only a small area of land is let on the conacre (eleven month) system. A typical farm consists of a narrow strip of land one field wide which includes some callow, some esker and some bog margin (fig. 11.7).

Fig. 11.7
"Lazy-beds" still visible on esker pastures provide evidence of previous spade cultivation.

Dry stock is still the principal system of farming and it is well suited to part-time management. Almost all the land (95%) is now in pasture with tillage rare, mainly because oats are no longer needed for horses. There are now half a dozen horses in the area compared with 160 in 1930. The crops sown include feeding barley, and turnips and potatoes are still common.

About half the pastures are used solely for grazing; the remainder are cut for hay, rarely silage. Tilled land being laid down to grass is reseeded with a standard grass/clover mixture, otherwise pasture land is rarely reseeded. The grass is managed by dunging and fertilizing with artificial manures and adding lime or lime-based fertilizers to wetland on the bog margin.

The grass is still grazed by young cattle brought in as calves and kept until they are 2 — 3 years old. A few farmers also keep sheep and sell their wool and lambs each year. There are a few herds of dairy cows but these account for only 5% of total cattle numbers. Dairying never expanded in Clonmacnoise even in the 60's and 70's and the nearest creamery is in Moate, 20 km north-east of Clonmacnoise.

CHAPTER TWELVE

Fin Lough

Daniel Kelly and Vera Power

INTRODUCTION

Ireland has many lakes but their distribution across the island is very uneven. Several of the southern and eastern counties have none at all and County Offaly has only four small lakes.

Fin Lough, 2-3 km south-east of Clonmacnoise and a short walk south of Mongan Bog, is a shallow lake which in winter covers some 16 hectares (fig. 12.1). In summer the water level falls and the area of open water shrinks; most of the "lake" changes to a green expanse of reed-beds and fen.

At this site we can see a range of wetland communities, from more or less aquatic, through a variety of fen types, to raised bog. The flora of this wetland is remarkably rich. To our astonishment, the botanists investigating the area listed some 197 species of flowering plants, of which six had never been previously reported from Co. Offaly. In addition we found 12 species of ferns and fern-like plants and 26 species of mosses. The fauna of Fin Lough is so far virtually unstudied, except for the birds (see Chapter 7).

The survival of this rich site is, as we shall see, something of an enigma. Fin Lough has changed much in recent times and its future is problematic.

Fig. 12.1
Fin Lough is bounded by
an esker ridge to the north
along which probably ran
an early road to
Clonmacnoise. In this
photograph (taken in 1973)
the monuments are outlined
against the Shannon.

ECOLOGICAL COMMUNITIES

The many kinds of plant are not scattered haphazardly through the area. Instead, we find particular species or combinations of species, occupying particular habitats. Whilst no two patches will be identical, we can recognise a series of ecological communities, changing gradually from the water's edge up to the margins of the drier wetland (fig. 12.2).

THE OPEN WATER

The depth of the lake in summer varies between 45 and 70 cm. The lake bottom is soft, varying from white marl (a mixture of clay and lime) to dark brown peat. The Irish name, Fionn Loch, means "white lake" and was probably given because of the colour of the underlying marl.

Even the open water is not devoid of plants. Some aquatic species grow completely submerged, often in dense beds. The principal species here are the Canadian pondweed

Fig. 12.2
The plant communities of
Fin Lough change gradually
from the water's edge to the
drier margins.

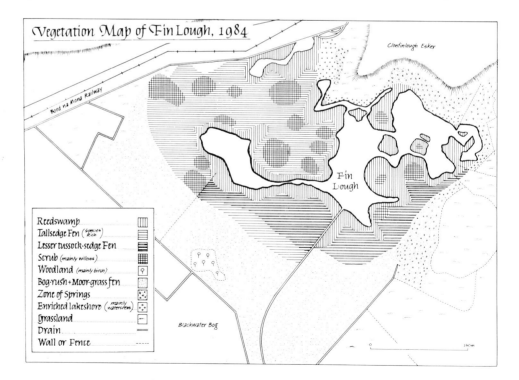

Vegetation Map of Fin Lough, 1984

Clonfinlough Esker

Bord na Mona Railway

Fin Lough

Blackwater Bog

Reedswamp
Tallsedge Fen (species rich)
Lesser tussock-sedge Fen
Scrub (mainly willows)
Woodland (mainly birch)
Bog-rush + Moor-grass fen
Zone of Springs
Enriched lakeshore (mainly watercress)
Grassland
Drain
Wall or Fence

and the stoneworts (*Chara*). The latter are robust green algae characteristic of lime-rich waters, and readily identified by their distinctive and disagreeable smell, reminiscent of garlic . Water milfoil and fennel-leaved pondweed are flowering plants that grow completely submerged; only their spikes of tiny, inconspicuous flowers stick up above the surface of the water. Other rooted aquatics have long-stalked leaves that float on the water surface: yellow water-lily, with its chunky flowers smelling of brandy, and broad-leaved pondweed. In a third group of aquatics, of which the duckweeds are an example, whole plants float freely. These are curious plants composed of flattened green "fronds", not differentiated into leaf and stem. The fronds accumulate near reed-beds, driven by the breeze and as its name implies duckweed is swallowed whole by ducks (fig. 12.3).

Many of the aquatic plants provide food for the waterfowl. For instance, mute swans can often be seen upending to graze the beds of fennel-leaved pondweed and other submerged aquatics in the centre of the lake. The lake supports a number of fish species: pike, rudd, perch, minnow and two kinds of stickleback. There is a rich insect fauna which includes lesser water-boatmen, water beetles, and juvenile stages of mayfly and dragonfly as well as *Coenagrion lunulatum* a rare damsel-fly. Snails, pea-clams and fresh water mussels are also common in lime-rich waters.

Fig. 12.3
The ivy-leaved duckweed has elongated fronds which grow in a tangle under the water surface.

Fig. 12.4
The plants which are found in the reed-beds around the lake are: the bullrush, easily identified by its spikes; club-rush, which grows in the deepest water, resembling a giant rush; and the common reed, tallest of all native grasses.

THE LAKE MARGINS

As we move to the lake margins where the water is shallower, one finds plants which, while rooted in the lake bottom, are able to send their shoots up into the air. Much of the lake is fringed by reed-beds 1.5-2 metres high. The principal species are (1) *Scirpus lacustris* (club-rush) forming dense, dark-green beds in deep water (a difficult

Fig. 12.5
In the reed beds one often finds the neatly plaited nest of a waterhen.

Fig. 12.6
Bogbean has creeping stems bearing leaves like giant shamrocks and in June spikes of pinkish-white flowers, the petals curiously fringed. The flowers are of two kinds, "pin-eyed" and "thrum-eyed", a feature also seen in primroses.

and dangerous community to explore!) (2) *Typha* (bullrush, reedmace or cat-tail) with its familiar cylindrical chocolate-brown flower-spikes and (3) *Phragmites* (common reed), tipped by flower-spikes like purple arrow-heads (fig. 12.4).

The tall reed-beds provide sheltered roosts for migrating birds; they are also a haven of privacy for nesting (fig. 12.5). Several species (for instance the moor-hen and coot) plait their nests from pieces of reed. The seeds of club-rush, spike-rush, bur-reed and sedges are important as food for wetland birds. The reed bunting and sedge warbler are two small birds whose names proclaim their fidelity to the wetland habitat. Both are frequent at Fin Lough.

Each year the reed-beds produce tall new growth and each year the old stems and leaves wither, fall into the water and decay. (We recall the poet Keats' evocation of winter: "The sedge has withered from the lake, and no bird sings"). On the lake bottom the supply of oxygen is low, and consequently the normal processes of decay are slowed down. Partially decomposed plant remains gradually accumulate to form the black or brown organic sediment known as peat. The process of peat accumulation and consolidation means that the water steadily becomes shallower and as a result different plant species can move in. We find a gradual transition from reed-beds to a fen community dominated by tall sedges.

THE FENLAND

A fen is an open wetland with a peaty soil which is rich in calcium and other bases. (see also Chapters 2 and 6). In winter the "tall-sedge"community is flooded by lake-water but in summer standing water virtually disappears although the ground remains waterlogged and more-or-less treacherous underfoot. The vegetation is composed of a rich mixture of species: principally sedges of many kinds (sixteen species of sedge have been listed from the wetland as a whole), water horsetail, water mint (you can smell the aromatic leaves as you walk) wild angelica, marsh pennywort, bogbean and many more (fig. 12.6). In shallow water to the south of the lake, behind the reedswamp we find beds of lesser tussock sedge (*Carex diandra*) and slender sedge (*Carex lasiocarpa*) with few associated species.

Scattered through the "tall-sedge" zone, we find stands of bushes or small trees, either willows (sallies) or birches. These stands are mostly of recent origin. The earliest

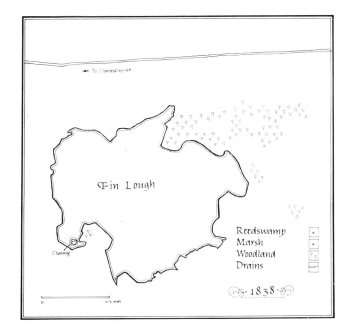

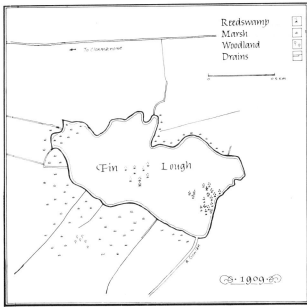

Ordnance Survey map shows only a tiny group of trees at the south-west corner of the lake (fig. 12.7). By 1884 a small but distinct wood had grown up at this site; it is still there today with little change in area. This wood is dominated by downy birch with willows mainly at the margin.

In the outer parts of the wetland area, the ground is relatively firm and is seldom flooded. Much of this drier fen is dominated by the tussocks of bog-rush and purple moorgrass, mixed with small sedges, and many other flowering plants. Spotted orchids (*Dactylorhiza*) are frequent, each flower-spike with a pink-and-white pattern which is slightly different from the next. Eight species of orchid are listed from Fin Lough. Orchids are plants which reproduce and spread slowly, and so can be easily wiped out by thoughtless flower-pickers. In late summer the beautiful and unusual ivory-white flowers of Grass of Parnassus catch the eye.

OTHER COMMUNITIES

To the south and west of Fin Lough we find a zone of transition from fen to bog. Beyond the farthest influence of the lake-water, the peaty soil becomes markedly acid.

Fig. 12.7
Changes at Fin Lough between 1838 and 1909.

Fig. 12.8
The leaves of bog myrtle smell like myrtle (a shrub from the Mediterranean) while the fruiting spikes smell of mangoes (a luscious tropical fruit!)

We find an intermingling of widespread species such as water horsetail and marsh cinquefoil with typical bog species such as heathers and bog-mosses (*Sphagnum*). Bog myrtle is locally abundant in this transition zone (fig. 12.8).

Yet another distinct ecological community is associated with the zone of springs just north of the lake, along the lower slope of Clonfinlough Esker. The spring water is saturated with lime: so much so that it precipitates out as a white deposit known as "tufa", encrusting the stones and mosses. The low, open vegetation is dominated by mosses and small sedges, together with bog pimpernel, marsh pennywort and the familiar daisy. Lime-loving stoneworts (*Chara*) grow in the permanent seepage streams which trickle down from the springs to the lake.

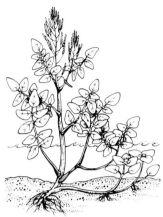

Fig. 12.9
Watercress sandwiches are much appreciated by the discerning palate....

This northern lake-shore differs from the rest in sloping sharply upwards. Along this shore, between the highest and lowest lake-levels, we find patches of a lush, juicy-looking vegetation quite different from any yet mentioned. Here are thick beds of the familiar watercress, (fig. 12.9) accompanied by fool's watercress (*Apium nodiflorum*; unrelated and inedible!). One also finds two unusual species, celery-leaved crowfoot (*Ranunculus sceleratus*) and water whorl-grass (*Catabrosa*). This unusual assemblage of plants points to a localized concentration of nutrients, phosphorus in particular. It seems clear that the principal source is the "guano", or faeces, deposited by birds, especially by the large colony of black-headed gulls which nests close by.

THE CHANGING LOUGH : THE NATURAL SUCCESSION

Fin Lough represents a remarkable survival, giving us some idea of how much of the region must have looked before the enveloping growth of the raised bogs. Deep borings taken from the centre of nearby Mongan Bog show at the bottom lake marl, then reed peat, then fen peat, and then a transition to bog peat dated to about 3500 years ago. At Fin Lough, we can see side-by-side the whole spectrum of these wetland communities.

The pattern of communities is clearly far from static. One community is replacing another through the course of time, the process known to ecologists as succession. In this lake basin, succession comes about primarily through the gradual accumulation of sediments: as the peat level rises relative to the water level, one plant community replaces another. We can see this particularly well from an aerial view: the reed-bed front is pushing out into the open water, like colonies of mould spreading over the surface of a jelly; the "tall sedge" community is spreading into the reed-beds on the landward side; willows and birches are overtopping the sedges, forming patches of incipient woodland. The appearance of previously non-existent stands of tree growth is particularly striking evidence that the vegetation around Fin Lough is in a state of flux.

Why has the process of succession not proceeded everywhere to the ultimate stage of the sequence? In other words, why has Fin Lough not vanished long ago, transformed into an arm of Blackwater Bog? Part of the answer lies in the presence of the zone of springs, coming out of the lime-rich esker to the north. The constant influx of alkaline water slows down the rate of peat formation and counteracts the acidifying process that is essential to the succession from fen to bog.

FIN LOUGH AND MAN

Human influences on Fin Lough probably go back far into the past but our historical information is limited. A crannog (fig. 12.10) was noticed at the south-west corner of the lough by the Geological Survey in 1884. In recent centuries the lake was a source of marl which had two uses: it was spread on land as a source of lime, and burnt for building mortar. In the early nineteenth century the lake was described as abounding with fish, especially eels, pike and perch. However, in the course of nineteenth-century drainage operations the Gowlan River, which drains the lake was canalized into a straight channel (fig. 12.11). The only connection with the Shannon today is by straight, deep bog drains inimical to fish life.

Fin Lough declined considerably in area between 1838 and 1909 compare figs. 7 and 11. The exploitation of the adjacent bogs by Bord na Mona, brought about further changes in recent decades. A series of deep drains were dug which have lowered the

Fig. 12.10
Crannógs offered protection for people and livestock against wolves and unfriendly neighbours. The location of its submerged trackway was known only to its occupants and invited guests.

Fig. 12.11
Fin Lough in 1984.

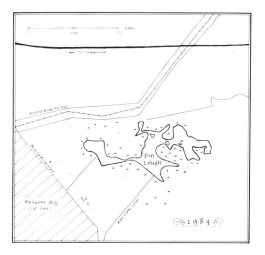

general water level (the watertable) over a wide area. One effect has been that Lough Nanag, the other, smaller lake in the Heritage Zone (see page 88) has virtually dried out in the past 15 years. Another side-effect has been the influx of peaty water into Fin Lough; suspended peat particles have settled out on the lake bottom, blotting out the white marl which gave the lake its name, and presumably causing big changes to the aquatic fauna. The lowering of the water table and the influx of peaty material from outside have combined to accelerate the natural succession: to reduce the depth and extent of open water.

Other human activities in the surrounding lands may have effects in the future. A striking change in the past few years has been the intensification of farming in the vicinity. Along with scrub clearance, ploughing and re-seeding of pasture, this involves increased application of chemical fertilizers rich in nitrogen and phosphorus. It is important that the lake-water be protected from pollution by excess influx of nutrients draining in from fertilized land. (The pollution of lake-waters by effluents from intensive farming is a severe problem in other parts of Ireland: Lough Sheelin is a notorious example).

To conclude, Fin Lough is a site of considerable scientific importance and enormous educational potential; it provides another unique element in the kaleidoscope of habitats that make up the Heritage Zone; its ecology is insufficiently understood, and its future is far from secure. We suggest that its conservation should be a matter of priority.

○
Vera Power is a research student in the Botany Department of Trinity College.

CHAPTER THIRTEEN

Conservation and 'The Clonmacnoise Heritage Zone'

David Jeffrey

WHO CONSERVES WHAT?

If you look up all the ways in which conservation is carried out in Ireland, you will not find 'Heritage Zones' mentioned. What is a "Heritage Zone" and how does it differ from other units of conservation? The term was invented by our study team from Trinity College in a report to the E.E.C. in 1984.

We stated: "A Heritage Zone (H.Z.) is a defined area with a sufficiently rich inventory of heritage items to warrant a concerted and co-ordinated approach to conservation."

This definition may be contrasted with the following units:

A NATIONAL PARK is a large unit of landscape, conserved for the benefit of the nation as an amenity and for nature conservation. The national parks are at Killarney, Co. Kerry; Connemara, Co. Galway; Glenveagh, Co. Donegal and one is being developed in the Burren, Co. Clare. Agriculture or other economic activity is not encouraged within the Parks although it is clear that they act as magnets for tourists. The land is owned by the State.

A NATIONAL MONUMENT is a work of man of cultural interest, usually of archaeological, historic or artistic importance. Some are State owned but most are in private ownership. In the Clonmacnoise area, the National Monuments are the

Clonfinlough Stone; the Monastic settlement in Clonmacnoise and its associated artifacts. The major national monuments (for example New Grange, the Rock of Cashel and Clonmacnoise) attract many visitors.

National parks and national monuments are administered by the Office of Public Works.

Under the Wildlife Act (1976), the Minister for Fisheries, Forestry and Tourism can declare an area a NATURE RESERVE in order to ensure comprehensive habitat protection. Most are State owned but the first declarations of privately owned reserves have recently been made. In either case, clear objectives for management must be set down. Potential nature reserves in the Heritage Zone are Mongan Bog, Finlough and the Rocks of Clorhane.

The Wildlife Act also provides for areas designated by the Minister as REFUGES FOR FAUNA. This extends the older idea of 'bird sanctuaries' and essentially means 'no shooting', rather than habitat protection.

Particular species and their habitats are scheduled for protection under the Wildlife Act and a number of these occur in the Heritage Zone e.g. the marsh pea and Greenland white-fronted goose

Under the Planning Acts, a local authority can seek a declaration from the Minister for the Environment for a SPECIAL AMENITY AREA ORDER, which gives an area special protection. The formula for this declaration is so complex that no successful cases have yet been made.

More general habitat protection of sites of scientific importance can be ensured through the use of CONSERVATION ORDERS under the Planning Acts administered through a local authority. A local authority can also make 'TREE PRESERVATION ORDERS' in response to requests from the public.

Without any legal standing, UNESCO has proclaimed two areas of Ireland "WORLD BIOSPHERE RESERVES", namely North Bull Island, in the City of Dublin and the Killarney Valley, Co. Kerry. Individual land owners can, of course, protect habitat by their own actions in implementing appropriate management.

The first matter which becomes clear from this litany of conservation units is that responsibility is divided. The second is that all conservation, as defined, is separated from economic activity, such as agriculture and tourism. Education in its broadest sense is given a very low key role, although 'interpretation' is making a welcome appearance at some national monuments and national parks and as a result of local initiative e.g. North Bull Island, the Burren, Roscrea Heritage Centre.

The idea of the Heritage Zone overcomes these drawbacks. In a defined area, all agencies having conservation interests could be permitted and encouraged to co-ordinate their efforts (fig. 13.1). On the one hand, this would lead to economies of scale in the technical and administrative aspects of conservation in terms of wardens, workforce, guides etc. On the other hand, the effect of the Zone in terms of tourist potential, educational and amenity value would be much greater than the sum of its parts.

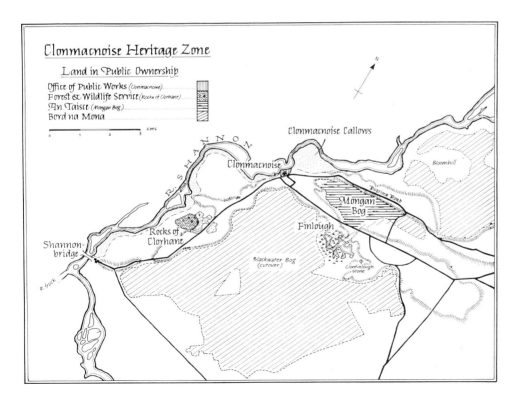

Fig. 13.1
Managing all the publicly-owned land for conservation would make a significant contribution to the development of the Heritage Zone.

SOME CONSERVATION DETAILS

At the National Monument in Clonmacnoise, all can see that conservation is an active process, requiring management and resources. The artefacts and physical structure of the monastic buildings are protected; visitors needs are met and a basic interpretation programme operates.

Conservation management will entail different operations at the other sites but the principal aims will be the same (fig. 13.2).

At Mongan Bog, it is extremely important to maintain the wetness of the bog and to prevent fire. Neither of these can be achieved without resources and the assistance of adjacent landowners and the public at large. The bog is greatly in demand for research but it is not properly accessible for educational purposes.

Fig. 13.2
Without extending the amount of land in public ownership, steps could be taken to develop the amenity and educational potential of the Zone.

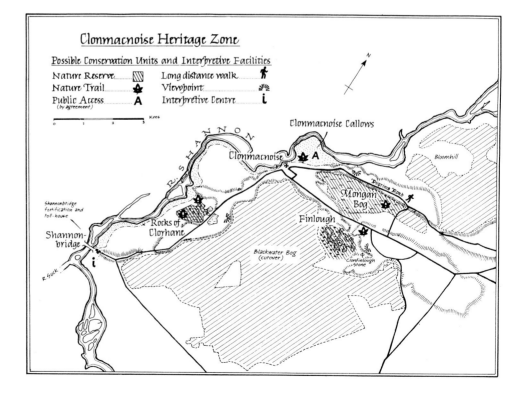

Much needs to be done for this site alone and a key part of a nature conservation plan is the appointment of a warden, as the bog must be monitored continuously.

The other two sites with similar management and interpretation problems are "The Rocks of Clorhane" and Fin Lough. The 'Rocks' case seems straightforward and a programme for management could be based on experience elsewhere. A simple nature trail along forestry tracks would provide access for interested visitors.

Fin Lough is so complicated that all aspects of management will not be totally refined for some years to come. This should not paralyse efforts for conservation as one can proceed by a series of approximations using the advice of engineers and hydrologists. For example, a key issue is the stabilisation of the water regime. This means preventing low summer conditions and avoiding undue flooding with acid water in winter. Local changes may have been caused by the construction of the Bord na Mona railway and a new agricultural regime on the eskers. These need monitoring and it is possible that any effects will be transient.

Interpretation of Fin Lough and Mongan Bog can be done together because of their proximity and inter-relationships. At both sites it will be desirable to design and engineer walkways to take visitors into the sites with minimum impact. These sites are as fragile as Skelig Michael and deserve as much care and attention.

The Heritage Zone has three other assets which are as much a product of the present management system as the natural environment: namely the River Shannon, its callows and the esker grasslands. The present system of management (barring loss of woodlands) seems to generate a rich pattern of wildlife. However, we do not understand precisely how this has occurred and there is no room for complacency. There is a need for greater levels of interpretation and these might be very directly related to tourism. Research must continue into the triangular relationship between conservation, agriculture and tourism.

The integration of conservation with agriculture is seen as being in the best interests of all parties. In the Clonmacnoise case, agricultural practice already contributes to the character of the callows and grasslands. On the other hand there could be significant seasonal income for those engaged in part-time farming, in conservation and amenity linked activity and in tourism.

FIRST STEPS

In the case of the Clonmacnoise Heritage Zone, two of its most significant qualities are the peace, and 'unspoilt nature' of the landscape. This quality appeals to the casual visitor, the pilgrim, the artist, the historian, those who fish and those who watch birds or study nature The residents also benefit from this atmosphere and all who care for the landscape realise that this could be a first casualty of foolish development.

However, by taking small steps and monitoring their consequences, it is likely that good conservation, development of a valuable educational resource and creation of income from tourism can all march together.

If the ideals of the Heritage Zone proposal are to be promoted a small management team needs to be set up. The team would carry out an agreed programme of conservation and education in harmony with the needs of agriculture, tourism and amenity. Local, regional and national guidance would be available to the team. It is arguable that this is an experiment which we cannot afford to miss.

Index

Suggestions for further reading

Chapter 1.

Herries Davies, G.L. and Stephens, N. 1978. *Ireland.* Methuen, London.

Mitchell, G.F. 1986. *The Shell Guide to Reading the Irish Landscape.* Country House, Dublin. (also Chapters 2, 8, 11).

Sugden, D.E. and John, B.S. 1976. *Glaciers and Landscape.* Arnold, London.

Chapter 2.

Edwards, K.J. and Warren, W.P. 1985. *The Quaternary History of Ireland.* Academic Press, London.

Moore, P.D. and Webb, J.A. 1978. *An Illustrated Guide to Pollen Analysis.* Hodder and Stoughton, London.

Chapter 3.

Hughes, K. and Hamlin, A. 1981. *Celtic Monasticism.* The Seabury Press, New York.

de Paor, M. and L. 1961. *Early Christian Ireland.* Thames and Hudson, London.

Ryan, Rev. J. 1973. *Clonmacnois — a Historical Summary.* Stationary Office, Dublin.

Cone, P. 1977. *Treasures of Early Irish Art; 1500 B.C. — 1500 A.D.* Alfred A. Knopf, New York.

Chapter 4.

Monahan, J. 1886. *Records Relating to the Dioceses of Ardagh and Clonmacnoise.* Gill and Son, Dublin.

Sheehy, J. 1980. *The Rediscovery of Ireland's Past: the Celtic revival 1830-1930.* Thames and Hudson, London.

Chapter 5.

de Buitleir, E. (ed.) 1985. *Irish Rivers.* Amach faoin Aer, Dublin. (Also Chapter 6).

Anon. *Wetlands discovered.* Forest and Wildlife Service, Dublin. (Also Chapters 6, 8, 11).

Baldock D. (ed.) 1984. *Wetland Drainage in Europe* (Chapter 3 on Ireland). IIEP/IIED, 10 Percy Street, London W1P ODR.

Chapter 6.

Nicholson, S. 1839. *A Report on the General State of Agriculture in the District of Country Adjoining the Middle Shannon.* Graiseberry and Gill, Dublin. (available in the National Library, Dublin).

Chapter 7.

Trodd, V. 1980. *Birds of Brosnaland.* County Offaly Vocational Education Committee.

d'Arcy, G. 1981. *The Guide to the Birds of Ireland.* Irish Wildlife Publications, Dublin.

Hutchinson, C. 1977. *Ireland's Wetlands and Their Birds.* Irish Wildbird Conservancy.

Chapter 8.

Bellamy, D. 1986. *Bellamy's Ireland: The Wild Boglands.* Country House, Dublin.

O'Connell, C. 1986. *The Future of Irish Raised Bogs.* No. 7, The Resource Source, Environmental Awareness Bureau, An Foras Forbartha, Dublin.

Fairley, J.S. 1975. *An Irish Beast Book: a Natural History of Ireland's Furried Wildlife,* Blackstaff Press.

Chapter 9.

Van Eck, H. Govers, A., Lemaire, A. and Schaminee, J. 1984. *Irish bogs: a case for planning.* Catholic University, Nijmegen, Holland. (available free from Citroenvlinderstraat 45, 6533 SX Nijmegan).

Evans, E.E. 1957. *Irish Folk Ways.* Routledge and Keegan Paul, London.

McCracken, E. 1971. *Irish woods since Tudor times.* David and Charles, London.

de Buitleir, E. (ed.) 1984. *Wild Ireland.* Amach faoin Aer, Dublin.

Rackham, O. 1986. *The History of the Countryside.* J. Dent and Sons, London.

Chapter 11.

Bell, J. and Watson, M. 1986. *Irish Farming, 1750-1900.* John Donald, London.

Sheahan, J. 1978. *South Westmeath: farm and folk.* Blackwater Press, Dublin.

Chapter 12.

Halliday, G. and Malloch, A. 1981. *Wildflowers — their Habitats in Britain and Northern Europe.* Peter Lowe, London.

Woods, C. 1974. *Freshwater life in Ireland.* Irish University Press.

Chapter 13.

Anon. 1981. *Areas of scientific interest in Ireland.* An Foras Forbartha.

Glossary

Arctic-alpine plants
plants which are found both in the alpine zone of mountains and the tundra areas of the north e.g. bog rosemary

Arterial drainage
straightening and deepening of river courses to reduce flooding and to allow better drainage of bordering farmland.

Clay minerals
The most finely divided soil particles which affect the structure and water-holding properties of soil and represent a reservoir of some mineral nutrients.

Corer
A tubular sampler for obtaining specimens of soft sediments or peat from a specific depth.

Epiphytic lichens
Lichens which grow on plants using them as a support.

Evapotranspiration
Loss of water from an area of vegetation combining evaporation from leaves via stomata and that from other exposed surfaces.

Manaig
lay workers who lived a semi-religious life with their families near the enclosure and who were probably descendents of the original landowners.

Microclimate
The special climate of an area where some particular feature results in a different climate from that of the surroundings.

Mycorrhizal fungi
Fungi associated with the roots of plants which assist nutrient uptake by plants in exchange for sugars.

Palynology
The study of vegetation cover in the past by examination of plant fossils such as pollen grains or seeds or larger pieces of plant material.

Peaty gley
A type of soil which has no easily distinguishable horizons and where dead plant material has accumulated on its surface as a result of periodic water logging.

Radiocarbon dating
A small proportion of the carbon in the atmosphere is naturally radioactive, and so the carbon incorporated into living material becomes similarly radioactive. When a plant dies no fresh carbon is incorporated and the radioactive carbon decays, halving in amount every 5500 years. A measure of the radioactive carbon remaining today tells us how many years have passed since the plant was alive.

Water table
The depth beneath the surface of soil at which it is permanently saturated with water.

Acknowledgements

The information in our book is principally distilled from studies carried out by the authors. Other individuals were involved in research at Clonmacnoise and thanks are due to those researchers whose results we shared and whose work has contributed to our understanding of the Zone. These include Jervis Good, Ken Bond, Michael de Courcy-Williams, Paddy Ashe, Des Higgins and Neil Lockhart.

The pleasure of doing research in this area was greatly increased by the help and hospitality received from the people of Clonmacnoise and Shannonbridge. We would like to thank everyone who facilitated our research.

Our gratitude is offered to the individuals and organisations who permitted the reproduction of photographs and drawings. These included: the National Museum (Figs. 2.6, 2.8, 3.9, 3.13, 3.15, 3.16, 3.17 and plate 8), the Society of Antiquaries (Figs. 1.7 and 4.7), the Office of Public Works (Figs. 3.18, 4.3, 4.8), the National Library (Figs. 4.2, 4.6, 11.4), the Royal Irish Academy (Fig. 4.1, Plate 8), Bord na Móna (Figs 8.13, 8.15, 9.1, 9.4, 9.5), the Board of Trinity College (Fig. 4.5), the Electricity Supply Board (Fig. 9.7), Herbst Engineering (Fig. 9.3), Cambridge University (Fig. 12.1), the Emerald Star Line (Fig. 5.6), Michael Heffernan (Fig. 3.5), Maptec Irl. Ltd. (plate 1), Oscar Merne (plates 2, 4, 5, 6, 7), Ingemar Lext (plate 2), James Gardiner (plate 7), Fota House, Co. Cork (plate 8) and Brian Madden (plates 3 and 4). Thanks also to George Sevastopulo and Thaddeus Breen for source material on which Figs. 1.2 and 2.7 were based.

Most of the book was typed by Norah Crummy whose expertise was invaluable. In the later stages the typing was done by the equally efficient Cathy Dawson. The text was proof-read by Michael Tubridy.

All maps are based on the Ordnance Survey by permission of the government (permit no. 4730). The aerial photograph of the Clonmacnoise area (Fig. 9.8) was obtained from the Ordnance Survey and reproduced with government permission (permit no. 4742).